AROUND THE WORLD IN
THE CINEMAS OF PARIS

AROUND THE WORLD IN
THE CINEMAS OF PARIS

THEODORE DALRYMPLE

MIRABEAU PRESS

Published by Mirabeau Press

PO Box 4281

West Palm Beach, FL 33401

ISBN: 978-1-7357055-0-7

First Edition

MIRABEAU

CONTENTS

PREFACE TO AN INTRODUCTION

When I finished this book, I little thought that it would be about a simple pleasure of the past, that my journey round the world in the cinemas of Paris would not again be possible, at least not for a long time, or perhaps ever. Even if the little cinemas that I haunted for a year, with their tiny sub-economic audiences, re-opened as normal, the atmosphere would be changed if not permanently, at least for a long time. Until amnesia works its magic, we shall look on people sitting near us, especially if we happen to be of a certain age (as I now am), as the potential bearers of the modern plague, Covid-19, and thus the harbingers of our death. We shall now consider, at least subliminally, an excursion to the cinema, which we once took without a second thought, as potentially dangerous, and the auditorium as a charnel house. We shall watch films with masks on, as if they emanated a poisonous gas, and while our fears will no doubt be grossly exaggerated, we are not so constituted as to fear risks strictly according to their statistical likelihood.

This book, then, was written in that happily naïve pre-Covid era when people assembled without a second thought. It was never intended to arouse nostalgia, as it might do now.

INTRODUCTION

Paris is the best city in the world for cinema (at least the best city in the world known to me), by which I mean there is a greater variety of films from around the world to be seen there than anywhere else.

It is only appropriate that it should be so, for it was in Paris that the Lumière Brothers first showed moving pictures to a public audience. In any case, film as an art has always been more highly regarded in France than in the English-speaking world, especially by intellectuals. In England, a cinema is a music hall, in France a library.

If you go to the cinema on your own in England, you are regarded as peculiar and slightly sinister: a paranoid schizophrenic, perhaps, or a sexual pervert. I remember in England once going to an art cinema, the kind that is patronised, if at all, by a small band of stalwarts, showing films of the kind of impenetrable obscurity that some mistake for profundity. On this occasion, however, it was showing a film with the simple, self-explanatory title, *Necrophilia*, made (if I remember aright) with the financial assistance of the Arts Council of Canada or Quebec. At the time I was writing a series of articles about the unusual pastimes of my compatriots, which is why I went. My wife came with me, somewhat reluctantly. The cinema was distinctly run-down — it has long-since closed — and very dusty. We seemed to be the only audience for this film until a man in an old gabardine raincoat, the very stereotype of the imagined lone cinema-goer, entered, looked round and, with the rest of the auditorium empty, sat next to us. This seemed to us creepy enough, though we were far too polite to ask him to move somewhere else, but when the title of the film appeared on the screen, he relaxed and sighed, like air escaping slowly from a balloon, 'Ah, necrophilia!'. My wife did not stay long: the film, which seemed to be state-sponsored propaganda for this harmless practice, combined with its evident aficionado were too much for her. She waited for me in the lobby, where I did not keep her waiting long.

In Paris, by contrast, it is perfectly normal for people to go to the cinema on their own, even — or perhaps especially — at the strangest times. They are neither schizophrenics nor perverted but artistic intellectual types (some might say all the more dangerous for that). The French savour films as they savour food.

Once, when my mother-in-law who lives in Paris had an operation requiring convalescence, my wife stayed by her bedside for a week. I visited often, but also went to the cinema twice a day, choosing films from obscure countries — obscure, that is, to the people who did not live in them — in which you would not normally have expected films to be made (for example, Guinea-Bissau). I discovered that they were usually a great deal more interesting, to me at any rate, than more commercial offerings, and it occurred to me that you could effect a voyage round the world without ever leaving the confines of cinemas in Paris. And this is what I decided to do.

To pursue my journey, I had often to go to a small cinema at eleven in the morning or at night, for the films that I wanted to see were shown only once or at a time that clashed with another film that I also wanted to see.

I chose the films by the location in which they were set rather than by their supposed quality. I did not want to step into the same river twice, as it were, by seeing a film from a country I had already visited cinematographically. I excluded films from France, Britain and America, as the countries were too familiar to me. Perhaps I am exceptionally gifted with the capacity to suspend disbelief, or too credulous, but in very few cases did I find it impossible to absorb myself in the film I was watching. I have written about them in the order in which I saw them, rather than put them in an order suggesting a coherent journey round the world.

Many of the films were from countries that I had visited or travelled through, though I did not know them well, and this gave me a different pleasure, that of nostalgia. But overall, I had no design: I chose films that happened to be showing when I visited Paris.

Being no enthusiast of the culture of stardom, I have mentioned no names apart from those of the directors. It was the depiction of the countries that interested me, and the reflexions that the films provoked. There was none that failed altogether to bring at least some grist to my mill of thought. At least, I hope that the reader will agree.

1

BRAGUINO, DIR. CLÉMENT COGITORE, RUSSIA

Most people, I suppose, have dreamt at some time of a simpler life, a life closer to nature: that is to say a life without tax demands, insurance bills, forms to fill, shopping to do, clothes to wash, finding a parking space, and all the other tasks that modern life imposes on us. Most such dreams, or daydreams, involve a tropical island where ever-ripe fruit grows in abundance on trees, fish can be scooped from the water by hand, the temperature is ever-equable, and so forth. They do not usually involve the Siberian taiga or include the struggle to keep clean, dry or warm.

In this short film of fifty minutes, however, a family, the Braguines, has made its home deep in Siberia, far from anyone else — except, that is, the Kilines, another family that has followed suit. There is no road to their settlement, which can be reached only by a very long walk, by river (it is on a tributary of the Yenisei) or by helicopter. The Braguine patriarch arrived forty years ago — in Soviet times, then — and constructed a cabin for himself. Although there is nothing in the film to suggest his deep, or even superficial, religious faith, he is an Old Believer, a follower of the Orthodox schismatics who rejected the Patriarch Nikhon's reforms of the Russian Orthodox Church in the Seventeenth Century. Braguine, after whom the settlement in named, is like the Cossacks who fled the Tsarist autocracy in order to be free; Siberia is large enough, evidently, for him to have escaped the Soviet yoke.

Now married, he has a brood of small children, all born in the taiga. He rejects the modern world in its entirety with its false and shallow values. He wants to live in communion with nature and his aim is to live in autarky, though he still has a boat with an outboard motor, and I doubt that he drills for and refines the necessary fuel for himself. Where does he find the fuel, and how does he pay for it? Questions like this recurred to me all through the film; I felt a little like the man who goes to Versailles and wonders how they polish all the mirrors.

The film shows the taiga in all its immensity, a wilderness barely imaginable to modern man who, however multicultural he may be, is as firmly enclosed in his own little world as humans have been throughout history. And as soon as one sees the taiga from the ground rather than from the air — on screen, of course — one feels a strange kind of release or relief from the pressures of urban life. Gone are the foolish concerns over status or making a mark in society. How little do we actually need to live! Nineteen-twentieths, at least, of our possessions are extraneous, superfluous, unnecessary, and they rule us rather than we them. As Braguine, the protagonist, says, he will never tire of the inexhaustible beauty of the taiga, which is itself a sufficient reward for existence. It is foolish to enslave oneself to imagined necessities, material or otherwise.

Ah yes, the siren-song of the simple life, how often have we heard it and failed to pursue it for lack of courage! Braguine, in his self-constructed wooden cabin, albeit with a typically Russian mess all around it, is a free man in a way that I shall never be. No gas, water, electricity or telephone bills to pay, no e-mails to answer, no subscriptions to renew, no invitations from doctors to attend for screening procedures, no anxieties over the latest international crises that won't affect one in the least and that one cannot influence, no news, only the quiddity of daily life.

Braguine goes hunting. He hunts for his subsistence, but his subsistence is his pleasure. His young children pluck the ducks that he shoots; they talk to the dead birds and address them with endearments as they do so. You can approach no nearer to, or be more respectful of, nature than that. How lucky are the children to be so free of the pressures of modern urban existence, the pressure on them to be, or to appear, adult from the age of nine, the need to compare their possessions with those of their peers, and so forth. Whatever becomes of them in later life, they will have had an idyllic childhood to look back on with nostalgia.

Braguine and his oldest son hunt a bear. It is a huge, magnificent but lumbering beast, to me terrifying, for which one can feel only the greatest respect. They, father and son, shoot it and then skin it. They also decapitate it and place its head on a tree trunk while uttering a prayer for the repose of its soul.

My knowledge of and contact with bears has been limited. I had a teddy bear as a child, of course, and once, with a feeling of guilt, ate a bear stew in a restaurant in Bucharest. I was in the city to see an exhibition of portraits of the late dictator, Nicolae Ceausescu, several of which showed him with a semicircle of dead bears stretched out before him which he had supposedly tracked down and shot. In one of these portraits there were twenty-four such bears splayed out before him, an odd and to me appalling symbol of patrician authority in a man who also took pride in his proletarian origins and who in his career had supposedly always furthered proletarian interests. Almost certainly the bears, if he had shot them at all, had been tranquillised first, both so that they could not attack him and that he could not miss them. One didn't know whether to laugh or cry at this absurd imitation of the former aristocratic obsession with hunting. Life, said Horace Walpole, is a tragedy to him who feels and a comedy to him who thinks. In reality, it is, or ought to be, a tragicomedy.

Braguine obviously loves hunting, but he hunts to feed and clothe himself and his family (one of his children appears in bearskin shoes shortly after he has shot the bear). I have never hunted, except once in Africa in the Tanganyikan savannah. I did so in the company of an old British soldier, a squaddie, and a Pakistani immigrant. Both spoke fluent Swahili and both laid claim to bushcraft. One held the gun and the other the ammunition. For some reason that I now cannot remember, they had a furious quarrel and stormed off in opposite directions, thus separating the gun from its bullets. I went off with the Pakistani, who had the latter. If we had been charged by an elephant or attacked by a lion, all we could have done was throw bullets at it. Of this I was secretly rather glad, for when I saw an animal, even an ugly one such as a warthog or African wild dog, I experienced no desire whatever to shoot it, rather the reverse. After an hour or two wandering in the bush, we were reunited, as was the gun with its bullets. Now slightly ashamed of themselves, these two supposedly experienced hunters thought that I should have the joy of killing something, and we came across a little green snake curled up at the base of a tree. They insisted that I shoot it, though I had no wish to do so. I took aim as best I could and pulled the trigger. Afterwards, there was no sign or remnant of it: it was vaporised. I felt no triumph, only guilt. Even had the snake been a green mamba — a highly venomous species, though it rarely attacks man and in this case was minding its own business — I had, unlike Braguine, taken life pointlessly.

One of the things that I first noticed about the Braguine children, apart from their flaxen hair and filthier clothes than any to be seen in a contemporary slum (no picturesque peasant costume for them), was their rotten teeth, the most rotten I had ever seen in a child's mouth, so rotten in fact that they ruined their otherwise angelically beautiful faces as soon as they opened their mouths. As it happened, I had recently been to see an exhibition of Scythian art and artefacts at the British Museum, where there had been displayed the skull of an ancient Scythian, about two thousand five hundred years old. I had been struck by the perfection of its dentition, with neither decay nor the grinding-down of molars seen among sedentary vegetarians. The Braguines, then, must have had access to refined sugar, suggesting — along with the fuel for the outboard motor — less than full autarky. This was another how-on-earth-do-they-clean-the-mirrors moment.

As I have mentioned, the only other people living within a

radius of hundreds of kilometres were the Kilines, who had a similar brood of children. They lived in immediate proximity of the Braguines, despite (or because of) the immensity by which they were surrounded.

Far from co-operating in their beautiful but harsh environment, the Braguines and the Kilines are sworn enemies. Braguine says that so great is their enmity, in fact, that one day somebody will be killed. Of course, it will be the Kilines' fault when it happens, for they are not really people of the taiga at all, but more interlopers, occupants or exploiters. The Kilines, he said, spied on us, the Braguines, watched us and even had equipment to record our conversations in their cabin. (You can take a man out of the Soviet Union, but you can't take the Soviet Union out of a man.) The Kilines would report everything that the Braguines said to the authorities.

This put me in mind of a case of *folie à deux* that I once treated as a young doctor, in which a couple living in a concrete block of council flats became convinced that their neighbours and enemies, a harmless old West Indian couple, had developed an electronic thought-scanner that was able to read and print out their thoughts (like an old-fashioned telex machine) as they had them. Paranoia is an ineradicable potentiality of the human mind.

In the film, we see the children of the two families confront each other. By the age of three or four, the children are aware that the other family is their enemy, much to be feared and never to be trusted.

The Braguines and the Kilines squabble over the precise limits of their respective plots of land. It seems a profound commentary on human nature — no doubt intentionally so — that in so immense a space, and with no one within several days' journey by foot, the two families should quarrel over the precise location of a boundary. It is as if enmity were what gave meaning to life; as if, without it, Man would not know how to occupy or amuse himself or fill his mind. Here was the story of Cain and Abel in the Russian taiga.

At the end of the film, a helicopter arrives in Braguino, bringing some thuggish-looking people, oligarchs, who claim that it is they who have title to the land, and that both the Braguines and Kilines must clear out. There is no escaping the modern world.[1] As flies to wanton boys are we to the gods.

---

[1] A village called Braguino is the location of one of Chekhov's short stories, *The Wife*. Braguino is so called after the local landowner, Braguine. Whether any reference to this story is intended by the film I do not know. Braguine is a common Russian name.

2

ARGENT AMER (BITTER MONEY), Dir. Wang Bing, China

Argent Amer was shown in a cinema in the rue Champollion at 11 in the morning. Champollion, of course, was the decipherer of Egyptian hieroglyphics; I had arrived from the rue Orfila, who was the first toxicologist in the world.

The cinema was open but deserted, except for an elegant but intellectual middle-aged lady. We waited for some time. Then she asked me which film I had come to see.

'*Argent Amer*,' I replied.

This was a relief to her: it suggested that she had come to the right place after all, or at least that we had both made the same mistake. There was no notice of, or poster for, the film, though it had been advertised in the *Officiel des spectacles*. A notice did inform us, however, that *Salle 1* was unheated because of a breakdown in the heating system.

Eventually an employee of the cinema arrived, a couple of minutes before the film was scheduled to be shown. We asked her whether we could buy a ticket. Not from her we couldn't, she said.

She told us we would have to wait for her colleague who was just about to arrive, which turned out not to be true. The precise role or function of the employee who *was* present was difficult to work out; it seemed to consist of walking slowly round the entrance lobby, going into the little box office and coming out again, walking round the lobby once more, and disappearing through a door marked *Staff only*. We had managed to extract from her the information that the film was to be shown in *Salle 3*, if it were to be shown at all, information that she gave out as if it were a state secret. Anyway, it turned out to be misinformation; when finally we got to see it, it was in *Salle 2*. We might have sat for quite a long time in *Salle 3* had I not taken the wise initiative of peeking next door to find the credits coming up.

'A typical French welcome,' said the intellectual lady, and we had a good laugh.

Actually, I have found the French more polite, on the whole, than the British, though it must be admitted that when they are rude, it is on a positively Soviet scale. I remember, for example, when my wife — who is French, so this is not xenophobic — tried to buy some pins in La Samaritaine, the large department store in Paris. She found the pins she wanted and took them to the cashier to pay for them. This lady was the only member of staff to be seen on the whole floor, but she told my wife that she could not take her money until she had a docket from the pin and mercery counter.

'There's no one there,' said my wife.

The cashier shrugged.

'Can't you just take my money?'

'No.'

'Can you call your colleague, then?'

'No.'

The cashier had obviously attended the Leonid Brezhnev school of service. I had known friendlier Soviet waiters. My wife was infuriated.

'Who's your manager?'

'I'm not telling you.'

'What's your name?'

'I'm not telling you that either.'

She was as immoveable as Ayer's Rock. We retreated; short of violence, she was impregnable. My wife's only revenge was to leave the pins on the cashier's counter, but it was obvious that the cashier couldn't have cared less. A week later, La Samaritaine closed its doors for good, but whether it closed because of this kind of treatment of customers, or this kind of treatment of customers was the consequence of its forthcoming closure, I could not say.

The slab-faced lady in the cinema had eventually returned and without explanation taken up the place behind the ticket counter, but she could not give us tickets because she had no change. This seemed to cause her no particular distress, and she merely suggested that we could pay after the film, though I doubted whether she cared much whether we did or not. *Argent amer* indeed.

The film was a long documentary (two and a half hours) on the life of a few emigrants from Yunan to the city of Huangzhou to work there in one of its 18,000 clothes factories.

Two things about this film displeased me. The first was that the camera appeared to be hand-held and no attempt was made to steady it. Perhaps this was to give the finished product a rawness that would supposedly add to its authenticity; but having reached a certain age, I am increasingly susceptible to motion sickness, and can almost induce nausea in myself by simply thinking of being on a boat. I suffered from such sickness throughout the film; the sickness was authentic, but the authenticity was not. It was bogus authenticity.

The second displeasing thing was that the director appeared to me not to be fully conversant with the distinction between tedium in life and tedium in art. Chekhov is the poet of boredom, but he is never boring. The director seemed to think that a long sequence of a man leaning over a balcony and staring into the distance achieved a significance merely by prolongation.

Still, nothing that comes out of China can be entirely without interest.

My main response to the life shown was horror at the sheer ugliness of a certain kind of modernity that in many respects represents progress — not only in China, of course, but particularly marked there because of its headlong flight into it. This reaction is all the greater because I have in my mind a certain idea of China (as de Gaulle might have put it), namely one of extreme aesthetic refinement, a refinement so great that it often makes our civilization seem coarse or crass by comparison. When I am in Paris, I seldom fail to visit the Musée Guimet or the Musée Cernuschi, both given over to Asian art: but of course this way of understanding China or Asia is about as sensible as trying to grasp European life and history by visiting the Albertina in Vienna. There is more to life than art, whatever importance we — some more than others — attach to it.

Once they have moved to Huangzhou, the emigrants see nothing beautiful, nothing green, for months on end, just the cheap and garish products of helter-skelter industrialization.

The protagonists do not complain of this, of course: they have other, seemingly worse miseries to endure. It was Brecht who said, 'First grub, then morality,' though as one might expect of this appalling man, who as far as I can tell never did a decent or unselfish thing in his life, he was wrong. No doubt he would have said that absence of beauty was a minor consideration while people were trying to raise their material standard above subsistence; but still one is entitled to ask, if the appreciation of beauty is one of the aims, or at least the consolations, of life, what will life be like when the whole world has been smothered in ugliness. Will it ever be made beautiful again?

I should have been more appalled, perhaps, than I was by the conditions in which the internal emigrants work in their small factories turning out cheap garments for the world. The workers often start at eight in the morning and continue till midnight. They sleep in overcrowded dormitories with hardly more space than for a bed. Their pay is exiguous, if they receive it at all, and even the owners of the small factories (or rather workshops) have difficulty in turning a profit because there is always someone able to undercut them. It goes without saying that the work is boring and mindless: and surely there are few states of mind that being busy *and* bored at the same time.

I felt vaguely ashamed of the theorizing that I then did in my mind to lessen my emotional reaction to the distressful conditions that the film showed. Though I should have hated the workers' life for myself, yet they, the workers, presumably found it preferable to the life they would have had to endure if they had stayed at home in the countryside. As far as one could tell, they had not been coerced into migration, and such choice as was available to them existed only because the conditions in the city were as they were. To improve those conditions by decree was to risk eliminating the choice altogether, for there were other populations in the world able and willing to take up the baton of cheap sweated labour. This was the lesson that political economy, the dismal science of the Nineteenth Century, which was indeed dismal, taught.

A second thought occurred to me to assuage my guilt at enjoying the advantages of Chinese sweated labour (as every middle-class person in the west does), this time an historical consolation. The conditions of the migrant workers, horrible as they were, bore no comparison with those of the first industrialization in the world, that of England in the first half of the Nineteenth Century. One has only to read of the admirable official reports of the conditions of the English working classes in the 1830s — admirable, that is, for their frankness and honesty, their determination to disguise or extenuate nothing — to understand that the Chinese industrialization of today has been, by comparison, easy on the worker. This is not because human nature has improved in the meantime, that man is any the less willing to exploit man, but because human activity, thanks to technology, has become so much more productive. It is for this reason that the workers, however horrible and stunted their lives by comparison with my own life or those of the people whom I know, are not half-starved, cold or filthy as they would have been in England a hundred and eighty years ago. When (in the film) someone is knocked over in the street and injured, an ambulance comes for him, presumably to take him to hospital where he will receive more effective treatment than an aristocrat would have received two centuries ago.

Not, of course, that any of this would be known to or console the Chinese migrant workers. We measure our miseries by our own standards and expectations, not by those of our distant, or even near, ancestors. It is far harder to count our blessings than to dwell on our misfortunes.

China is a dictatorship and the Communist Party still has a monopoly of political power. But what was surprising — on reflection, not as an object of primary perception — was that the almost complete absence of the state or its officialdom in the lives of the people as portrayed in this film. Apart from a very brief discussion at the beginning of the film by would-be migrants of the difficulties of obtaining residency permits for Huangzhou (the very need for which tells you something in itself), neither political oppression nor official interference make themselves felt. There is more than one explanation for this, of course: that there was in fact no such oppression or interference, or that the film-maker thought it wise not to portray them if he wanted his film to be shown and to have permission to make further films. I am agnostic as to which is the better explanation, being too ignorant to judge.

Neither did industrial pollution, which in my brief experience of Chinese urban life is overwhelmingly evident, make any appearance in the film. But a film is a film, not an encyclopaedia of woes.

3

MAKALA, DIR. EMMANUEL GRAS, THE CONGO

The Congo, or Zaire as it was when last I visited in 1986, is not easily forgotten. I crossed it from east to west by what passed for public transport: a journey which I could not in safety make now. Progress is not a smooth upward curve.

I had since watched two films about the Congo in Paris cinemas, the first a Belgian documentary about the life of Mobutu Sese Seko, by the end of which, surprisingly, one feels a distinct sympathy for the sick, aging and defunct dictator, and the second a German documentary about a Congolese enthusiast who starts a symphony orchestra in Kinshasa. As so often, I was moved in this film by the spirit of the Africans in overcoming the most difficult conditions (admittedly many of Africans' making), all with a good humour that shames the European tendency to carp at the most minor inconveniences.

Makala, which I saw in a vast complex of 37 screens in a single cinema in Les Halles, a concrete mall in the centre of Paris where the youth of the Parisian banlieues seems to gather. Not long before, I had read an article in *Le Monde* describing how that youth, mainly of African or Maghrebin origin or descent, gathers there because it is more American in atmosphere (so said one of the writer's informants) than French. This I found depressing, because by *American* was meant the American *ghetto*, whose culture is one of the least attractive cultures, to me at least, in the world, consisting of irresponsibility, coarseness, violence, militant slovenliness and vile, brain-deadening music. It demands respect, by which it means fear. The reluctance of intellectuals to criticise it, or even worse the tendency to toady to it, for fear of being branded racist, suggests to me the deep uncertainty of many about their own inner feelings.

The protagonist of *Makala* is a villager in the Congo, not of the rain forest but of the savannah. We see him first in his village with his wife and young children, the eldest of whom has the protuberant belly of malnutrition and infestation by parasites. They live in a mud hut — of the kind familiar to me from my travels through Africa — to the interior wall of which is affixed an old and worn illustrated magazine, the only affordable decoration. There are practically no possessions or furniture. We see his wife roasting a rat over a fire, the only meat they have: a symbol both of the family's impoverishment and the denuding of the environment of its fauna. I remember very well in rural Nigeria the sale of what was called *bush meat* hung up for display on a kind of gibbet, rats and other rodents, all more substantial animals having been eliminated long ago by the over-hunting consequent upon the increase in population. One does not enquire, said Bismarck, how sausages or politics is made; in Nigeria, one did not ask from what animal the meat relish to give flavour to a starchy staple had come.

In the morning, the protagonist goes out with his axe and

after a long trek begins to fell a huge tree, the last such specimen still standing within a wide radius. The land has been as denuded of its trees as of its animals, and the protagonist cannot afford to notice or regret the beauty and magnificence of the tree: he sees only its potential to be turned into charcoal. He therefore cuts it down and then into pieces at the cost of many days — weeks — of backbreaking labour. With a chainsaw it would have taken a few hours at the most and required but a fraction of the effort. His toil is neither pleasant nor health-giving but incessant, unremitting and exhausting. At times we are unsure he can continue, so exhausted is he; thin and wiry, he has not an ounce of bodily excess or reserve.

Turning the wood into charcoal is another immense labour. He has to bury it in a mound of earth and then set fire to it, so that it smoulders rather than bursts into flame. This, one feels, will be the last of the charcoal in the area. *Makala* goes profoundly against the romanticization of the pre-industrial era, when Man was supposedly in harmony with his surroundings.

He and his wife, baby strapped to her back in typical African fashion, pack the charcoal into sacks which he then loads on to his old bicycle, or rather overloads it, as in another age a pack-animal might have been overloaded to death. His plan is to take the charcoal to the nearest town, more than thirty miles away, and sell it there. His dream, his ambition, is to buy with the proceeds some corrugated metal sheets with which to roof his home. His other dream or ambition is to plant fruit trees round his hut, oranges, apples and mangoes. The modesty, but also the decency, of his ambitions, whose achievement will harm no one, is touching in the extreme.

We see him setting off in the night with his heavy-laden bicycle which he pushes by means of an ingenious wooden arrangement. He travels at night to avoid the heat of the day. Every yard of progress is bought at the expense of immense effort: one sees the strain on his cable-like muscles. To steer the bicycle is a colossal undertaking for a man, but he is determined: he has a vision of a corrugated metal roof and has the welfare of his family constantly in mind.

How well I remember the roads in the Congo! I travelled a thousand kilometres along them, perched on the top of a loaded truck on which I had hitched a lift, along with other passengers. The roads were either dry, rutted and dusty, or muddy, all but impassable. It was said that the villagers along the way would, in the wet season, dig elephant-traps in them for any vehicle to fall into. Then they would demand payment for assistance in digging the vehicles out. When I went, it was still the dry season, but only just. We swayed and bumped and ground along very slowly (in bad conditions it could take a month to go the thousand kilometres), and we passengers could easily be shaken off the top of the load; I thought I was being heroic by enduring the discomfort of it, but it was the sheerest luxury by comparison with what the man with the charcoal endured.

We see him laboriously pushing his bicycle along what is little more than a laterite track until at last he reaches the main road to the town. This is much wider but hardly easier for him to negotiate. Vehicles now pass him from time to time, shaken into rattletraps by the corrugations in the surface, but damaged as they are (one would not have been surprised to see them suddenly disintegrate into a rusty pile of their component parts) they seem like arrogant manifestations of prepotent privilege as they pass him without slowing down to try to reduce the clouds of dust that they throw up and that smother him as in a dust storm. The Congo is no place for sentimentality.

Resting by the side of the road, somehow propped upright, his bicycle is knocked over by a passing vehicle that does not stop and whose driver either does not notice or does not care what he has done. We, who have seen the human cost of the protagonist's journey so far, are devastated on his behalf: it is the achievement of this film that we now see the world through the protagonist's eyes. Local people, whom he touchingly calls *mes frères*, my brothers, help him right his bicycle and repair it, so that he can continue his journey. We are immensely relived on his behalf, almost as if it were our own fate in jeopardy.

Traffic becomes heavier as he approaches the town, and then we see that he is not alone in his endeavour: there are many other peasants pushing similar bicycles with similar loads. At the entrance to the town is a roadblock, where a man of unidentified function or legal standing demands a large payment for permission to go further. No reason, no justification, is given for this exaction: here there is no why, to quote the guard at Auschwitz. It is an exercise of power, that is all.

The protagonist asks the man at the roadblock (*mon frère*) to take pity on him, for he is poor and has no money, but the man's reply is without appeal:

'Why should I take pity on you?'

In lieu of money, the protagonist has to hand over a sack of his charcoal, and we are filled with impotent rage on his behalf.

I remembered my entry into the city of Kisangani (the former Stanleyville) thirty years before. I was still perched on the top of the truck. There was a roadblock manned by soldiers to extort money from those who wished to enter. But the quality of the road had improved a few kilometres out of the city and instead of stopping, the driver of the truck accelerated as fast as he could, to the previously unimaginable speed of perhaps thirty miles an hour. He drove straight through the roadblock, the soldiers jumping along with fleeing chickens into the ditch by the side of the road to avoid being run over. I was terrified.

'They'll shoot,' I cried.

'Oh no, monsieur,' said one of my fellow-passengers calmly. 'They sold their bullets long ago.'

I was not surprised to hear that the Zairean army later collapsed without resistance in the face of a not very formidable armed rebellion. Its metier was extortion, not fighting.

The protagonist enters the town at last in which he hopes to sell his charcoal. The type of town was familiar to me also, a heaving mass of people in the main street, through which sway and swerve trucks and bicycles and buses and taxis and bullock carts, avoiding potholes and people, claxons squeaking or bellowing, the whole street or avenue or even boulevard (grandly-named) an anarchy of bar and brazier and bazaar. Rich market women in splendid turbans who carry thick wads of money bargain with mock outrage over the money offered for purchases, poor peasants spread their

24

pathetic produce before them on the ground which, even if sold, will bring them hardly anything (but they must think it worthwhile, otherwise they wouldn't do it, eloquent testimony to their grinding poverty). At night the bars and guest houses come into their own, throbbing with African popular music (to my ears infinitely preferable to our own rock music) and with a constant hum of the individual generators that anyone who desires electric light or power must have. There is also the sound of laughter and drinking, of animated conversation, and of prostitution practised without moral reprehension — though not, of course, without the dangers of infection. The towns are ugly, without grandeur or aesthetic interest, but they are profoundly human, so human in fact that I am both attracted and repelled by them.

The protagonist manages to sell his charcoal, though the money he obtains for it is insufficient to buy the sheets of corrugated metal that he hoped for. We see him buy medicine for his child at a pharmacy that sells the cast-off pills and potions of Europe, as well as the more or less useless patent medicines manufactured for the poor and credulous. By now I identify so strongly with the protagonist that I want to jump into the screen and tell him not to waste his money on buying kaolin to cure his child's diarrhoea, sold to him by a clearly crooked pharmacist (or owner of the wooden stall that poses as a pharmacy). I hope against hope that he will not be robbed on the way home of the money that remains to him from his prolonged, backbreaking labour.

Now freed of his physical burden, he begins his return journey. He begins by entering a Pentecostal church, an ordinary construction just like the others, in which people utter ecstatic prayer and weep and wail with the encouragement of a pastor of whose honesty one is far from convinced. But their faith gives meaning to their difficult lives and consoles them in their sorrows. The protagonist prays, but there is nothing extravagant in his prayer; it is a simple, moving and modest one, that with God's help he will be able to look after and provide for his family. We pray for him, too.

I am familiar with these ecstatic churches, which most intellectuals would sneer at as ridiculous though amusing. In Nigeria, I attended the services of the Eternal Sacred Order of Cherubim and Seraphim whose congregations dressed in white satin robes that did one's heart good to see. As it happened, I lived for a time in England round the corner from a chapel of this order in a disused school and saw the satin-robed congregants brighten the dull streets each Sunday morning. I stayed a week in a hotel in Coventry where I appeared as an expert witness in a murder trial, whose ballroom was used during the week as a chapel in which Nigerians gathered to raise their voices in praise of the Lord each evening. Coventry was, I discovered, a city of many Nigerian students, and strangely enough I felt more comfortable with them than with their English counterparts. They were better mannered, more civilized, less superficial, and I appreciated their humour and irony, their familiarity with suffering that was not self-inflicted, and their knowledge of the tragic dimension of life. I ate in a Nigerian restaurant where they gathered (the only one I have come across in England) whose proprietor asked me how I had come to like Nigerian food. I told her I had been to Nigeria several times and asked her whether she had many white customers.

'You are the first one,' she replied.

In Paris, I spoke of *Makala* to one of my mother-in-law's carers who was Cameroonian. She recognised at once the accuracy of the film: this was what it was like to live in Africa.

Makala moved me greatly. It showed both the brotherly solidarity and the pitiless exploitation of African life. It showed a man whose poverty could scarcely have been more grinding, unimaginable to us, and yet who remained good. By its end, we not only liked but admired him. His heroism was far greater, or at least more attractive, than that of the heroes of those violent films that attract large audiences.

As I watched him pushing his bicycle along the rutted laterite road, covered in dust by a passing car whose occupants would not have deigned to notice him, I thought back thirty years to the time when, in a broken-down small bus packed like a tin of sardines that ground its way along the red rutted road protesting like a wounded animal, a limousine shot past us at speed, throwing up choking clouds of dust in its wake. The limousine would not last long driven at such a pace along such roads, but it was obvious that there would always be another one where it came from. One of the passengers in the bus said, in matter-of-fact words forever engraved on my memory, '*C'est un grand.*'

They rendered all other words redundant.

4

THE SQUARE, DIR. RUBEN ÖSTLAND, SWEDEN

Sweden is very far removed, in more senses than one, from the Congo: but because the Congo is a land of miseries, it does not mean that Sweden is a country of felicity.

The Square is an unsatisfying film from the artistic point of view, at least for me on a single showing. It attempts too many things at once, from literal realism to satire, from surrealism to tragedy. But cinema is an art absolved from the need for perfection, and *The Square* has much to tell us of Sweden, and not only of Sweden.

The protagonist is the director of a fashionable 'cutting-edge' modern art gallery situated in a former royal palace. This location in itself tells us something significant: it is the triumph in modern society of the bourgeois bohemian over both the aristocracy and the traditional commercial *haute bourgeoisie*. Expensive casual is the new uniform of the powerful (in Amsterdam, only the taxi drivers wear ties).

The director is walking one morning in a busy Stockholm square after having just emerged from an underground station when he hears a woman screaming that she is under attack and in danger, calling on people to her aid. No one heeds her despite her increasingly desperate pleas for assistance: the passers-by are all too absorbed in the screens of their mobile telephones. They mind their own business in the worst possible sense of the words.

This is a none-too-subtle commentary, of course, on the individualism (without individuality) of modern societies, not just of Sweden. The real egotism of the Swedes is in marked contrast to the theoretical collectivism of their politics.

The woman under attack runs into the protagonist, apparently pursued by a man whom she suggests is trying to kill her. Another man seems to come to her assistance. Almost immediately, the woman runs off and the man who has come to her assistance lingers a short while to enjoy a moment of triumph and self-congratulation with his co-saviour, the director of the art gallery. But when the director continues on his way, he soon discovers that he has been relieved of both his wallet and his mobile phone.

This is a revealing or symbolic moment. There has probably never been a society more self-congratulatory than the Swedish, for it comes to the assistance of everyone. The director is suddenly awakened from his complacency, as was Dutch society by the murders of Pym Fortuyn and Theo van Gogh.

The director's life does not return to normal. That normality has already been shown to be based on what amounts to fraud, namely that of the art by which he earns his comfortable living. His gallery's current exhibition is of neat little piles of gravel arranged geometrically in a large room. When asked to talk about this art, he does so in such unintelligible gibberish that even the French audience in the cinema, well-used to incomprehensibility emerging from the mouths of intellectuals, laughed, as if at themselves. Such art is, of course, the plaything of those who more ardently desire to be artists than they have anything to communicate, or any skill with which to communicate it.

One of the director's young staff points out to him that, thanks to modern technology, the physical location of his stolen phone, and presumably of his wallet, can be traced. They then track it to a tower block of flats in a housing estate in the suburbs of Stockholm, where the population is largely immigrant. The director drives there with his assistant in his Tesla car and delivers a written message through each letterbox in the block that he knows the resident has stolen his wallet and his phone and demands that the thief return it to a convenience store at the local station, from which he will pick it up. In due course, the thief does return them, but at the same time a boy of about twelve or thirteen from the block traces him and begins to haunt him in a slightly menacing way. The boy thinks that, thanks to the piece of paper pushed through the letterbox, his parents have been accused of being thieves, and the boy eventually demands that the director go to his parents and apologize to them.

I don't know Sweden well, but this situation seems to capture rather neatly its conflicted attitude to the mass immigration that it has encouraged in late years. The director is clearly a member of the liberal intelligentsia who would, in theory, be favourably disposed to such immigration, largely on abstract humanitarian grounds. At the same time, however, he would normally have no personal contact with any of the immigrants, except perhaps as a cleaner or some other menial. Where the immigrants live is actually as foreign to him as any foreign country, and when the theft forces him to have an interaction, he discovers that, beneath his surface benevolence, he has precisely the same fears and prejudices about immigrants that he would normally have regarded as politically retrograde or worse.

Nor are these prejudices completely without foundation: after all, his phone and wallet *were* taken by people of the immigrant milieu. The problem is that he has accused everyone in the block of the crime, tarring them all with the same brush, though most of them are innocent of the crime. The fact that the majority of crime is caused by immigrants does not mean that the majority of immigrants commit crime. Here is the dilemma of the liberal conscience, which is usually resolved by denying that much of the crime *is* committed by immigrants or their close descendants.

The best way to resolve the dilemma, however, is to close down debate on the whole question, and (if my Swedish informants are correct and not exaggerating) this is the method the Swedes have favoured. Frank debate and open discussion are now almost impossible in Sweden and certain views or opinions have been all but criminalized. Openly to express these views or opinions may lose your employment, no matter how many people may secretly hold them. Some attempt to suppress them even in the privacy of their own thoughts and thus open yawning gaps between what is thought, said and felt. The more the auto-censorship is demanded or necessary, and the longer it lasts, the greater the sensation of living in a pressure cooker that will explode one day. Before that day, the auto-repression grows ever-stronger, ever more demanding.

On the immigrant side, things are hardly any better or more comfortable. Officially recognised, welcomed, granted rights, given benefits, etc., the immigrant knows that he is actually feared and disliked. He is the object of a cold and abstract, almost ideological, charity of the kind that it is demeaning and unpleasant to receive, though there is no alternative to receiving it. He is expected to feel grateful and loyal to people whom he knows perfectly well despise him in their hearts. Moreover, he has a little cognitive dissonance of his own to deal with. On the one hand he must protest against the stereotypical views of himself held by the host population, and on the other he must suppress knowledge that in part they capture a reality. The result is a kind of free-floating anger, manifested as a prickly insolence. That is why in the United States the partisans of the *Black Lives Matter* movement become so angry when it is pointed out that young black men are in far greater danger from each other than from any agents of the state, black or white: they know it is true but cannot acknowledge it openly, even to themselves.

Thus, *The Square* succeeds in capturing the curious and uncomfortable existential situation in Sweden, despite (or is it because of) its general prosperity and high level of education. If the film is not altogether an artistic success, it is because it does not amalgamate its various strands into a coherent whole, for example a largely irrelevant love interest. But one of its almost surreal scenes is important and powerful symbolically, even if it is not well-integrated into the whole.

In this scene, a rich bourgeois audience in evening dress has gathered for a gala dinner in a gilded hall. It is in aid of the director's gallery, and the diners are the great and the good. Laid on as an entertainment is the performance of a kind of ape-man, actually an ugly, stocky and powerfully built white man naked from the waist up. He prances round the dinner tables on all fours, peering closely at the guests like an ape. At first they take this as a joke, as the performance it is supposed to be; but gradually the ape-man becomes more and more menacing and aggressive. He knocks things off the tables, interferes with men and leers at women. The laughter becomes nervous and insincere. At what point do the assembled members of the bourgeoisie realise that this is no longer a performance but a real threat? It is astonishing how far one uncouth or uncivilized man can dominate, by behaving abominably, hundreds of cultivated, civilized people. For a long time — so the film conveys — they are paralysed by him, but then he goes too far. He actually starts to rape a woman in front of them, dragging her from her chair as she screams for help. First one man comes to her assistance, and then, in a flood, many others. They begin to beat the rapist savagely, and suddenly one sees their capacity for hatred and violence underneath their polished exteriors. They do not want merely to stop or restrain the rapist but to beat him to death.

The scene reminded me of Max Frisch's great play, The *Fire-Raisers*, which raises the question, perhaps unanswerable in a definitive way, of when tolerance of wrong-doing ceases to be tolerance and becomes pusillanimity or even complicity. At what precise point does one say 'Enough!' Great evils grow out of small beginnings, but not every small beginning grows to be evil. Therein lies the permanent need of judgment. The problem is compounded by the fact that if a great evil is averted, it cannot be known to have been averted. If Hitler had been assassinated early in his career, who would have known that Auschwitz had been averted? We can know what happened, more or less, but we cannot know what would have happened if what happened had not happened.

This scene in the film, besides being deeply disconcerting in itself, carries a disquieting symbolism for Sweden, and perhaps for the rest of Europe. The interloper, the ape-man, could be taken to symbolise the immigrant, at least the immigrant from a very different culture, who enters a complacently prosperous world and disrupts it, despite his type being a small minority. He behaves in a manner inimical to the decorum of the majority, or at least of the previously existent elite. Before long he evokes a savage reaction, bringing out or releasing forces that lurk under the most civilized of veneers. This film, then, might be said to express Sweden's otherwise inexpressible anxieties. The country is paying the price for its past moral grandiosity and conceit.

5

I AM NOT A WITCH, DIR. RUNGANO NYONI,
ZAMBIA

Zambia, the former Northern Rhodesia, is a country almost
without international profile, not since the downfall of its first
president and lachrymose dictator, Kenneth Kaunda, and is
certainly not associated in most people's minds, if associated
with anything at all, with film-making. Even Kenneth Kaunda
lacked those bizarre qualities that made the first generation or
two of African dictators after independence so interesting,
absurd and dangerous. He was only an averagely
incompetent, averagely corrupt, averagely Christian-socialist
kind of mission-educated, would-be philosopher-king. And
since his downfall, his country has been principally known for
nothing at all.

The landscape in which this film takes place captures this
dispiriting yet in some ways reassuring featurelessness: that is
to say, a seemingly endless non-descript savannah of trees
growing in laterite earth, with a few fields of maize in between.
Its sole grandeur is its extent; it is a landscape made for
mediocrity.

Yet everywhere is interesting, especially if inhabited; and in
the film we are shown the strange mixture of the pre-modern

and the ill-digested modernity that was brought into being in Africa by colonialism. The colonial period was brief, but its effects were irreversible.

Shula is a little girl of eight or nine who is walking in the bush behind a young woman who is carrying a pot of water on her head. The latter stumbles and falls, and the pot is broken. Anyone who has toiled at human porterage in the African sun, or merely witnessed it, will know how distressing such an event would be.

The little girl is a stranger in the village in which the woman lives, and no one knows where she comes from. She is immediately accused by the villagers of being a witch, and we see her being brought to the local police stations under that accusation. The villagers clamour for her removal from the village.

The lone policewoman (in a uniform that is clearly a legacy of the colonial era, her cap perched absurdly on her hair, her face heavily made-up), sitting behind her desk accustomed to doing not very much except possibly attempting some slight exaction from the local population, has no idea of how to respond to the popular clamour. She takes and takes some ludicrous and irrelevant evidence from the excited villagers. Still not knowing what to do, she takes out her mobile phone and calls her superior in the police.

We first see her superior, obviously a big man locally, lying in his bath being washed by a woman whom he orders about in peremptory fashion, peremptoriness being his manner of expressing authority. When his phone rings, he does not fetch it but, as a matter of principle, has it brought to him. He is, of course, very fat, his skin glistening with well-being, his size befitting a man of his importance, of which indeed it is the visible sign.

This is accurate. In very poor countries, obesity is of different, indeed opposite, significance from what it now is in the West, a sign of wealth rather than of poverty. I remember thirty years ago in Tanzania where, despite its egalitarian ideology, you could always tell a government man — a member of the *Chama Cha Mapinduzi*, the Party of the Revolution — by his girth. The peasants were thin, but the officials were fat. So great is our concern about the epidemic of obesity that we are apt to forget that for the vast majority of human history, in which subsistence was far from assured, being fat was associated with status.

The fat man tells the policewoman that she did well to call him. Thus, he asserts his importance. But though he dresses in expensive suits and ties, even in this middle-of-nowhere, and has a large colonial-style house furnished in best Third-World-baroque style, and his mobile phone is his constant companion as evidence of the world's need to be in permanent contact with him, he does not dismiss the accusation of witchcraft out of hand: on the contrary, he believes in it himself, and tells the policewoman that 'these witches' can be very crafty, concealing their true nature by their plausible denials of the accusations against them. That, he says, is what makes them so dangerous.

He orders Shula to be taken to a camp for witches. She has a choice: either to be kept there as a witch among other witches (who are much older than she) or be transformed into a goat, killed and eaten.

The witches in the camp are all secured to a post by a long

white ribbon to prevent them from flying away and doing harm elsewhere. They are taken out to work in fields on a flatbed truck on which posts are fixed and to which their ribbons are tied. We see the women, still tethered to the truck, working in the fields, weeding by hand, their labour tedious and backbreaking, indistinguishable from slavery. It is a powerful image and causes us to wonder to what extent we are all tethered by our circumstances. How many of us would do what we are doing if our choice were entirely free?

The important policeman, Mr Banda, makes use of the child witch to catch thieves, having assumed that she has special powers of divination. She points out the thieves in line-ups. Eventually, however, she is killed because she fails to make the rain fall in the midst of a drought (as she is assumed to be able to do) and on the contrary is suspected of prolonging the drought.

Like the Swedish film, *The Square*, this film is part social realism, part satire and part surrealism. There must be a fashion for this admixture, a fashion that does not please or convince me but which is nevertheless not without interest.

Luckily, the film was written and directed by an African, otherwise it would have been accused of colonialist apologetics or racism, for it is certainly an unflattering portrait of contemporary Africa, and not just of Zambia. The director of the film, Rungano Nyoni, did some research into a witch-camp in Ghana, very far from Zambia. She herself was born in Zambia, but her parents moved to Wales when she was five and she studied in England, where she has spent far more of her life than in Zambia. All the same, her Zambian background and descent protect her from the accusations that would be made against any European director of such a film, though no doubt some might accuse her of being prey to a kind of cultural Stockholm syndrome, in which she has adopted the worldview of those who oppressed her and her compatriots.

Not that she is altogether complaisant towards Europeans, who appear in the film in a very poor light. They have walk-on parts as tourists who are taken to the exotic witch-camp as a tourist attraction, where they take pictures of the tethered witches to show the family back home. Their curiosity is idle and condescending: they photograph the witches as they might photograph animals in a game park, and it scarcely occurs to them that the witches, so-called, are individual human beings rather than mere exhibits for their amusement.

In an article in the *Guardian* newspaper about Rungano Nyoni, she is reported as saying that she is agnostic as to the reality of witchcraft, which I would interpret (though I may be wrong) as meaning that, in her heart, she believes in its reality, for if she did not she would simply say so. But, rather curiously, she said that she wanted by her film to draw attention to the fact that camps for witches in Africa, which really do exist, are inhabited only by old women and young girls — as if they would be better if they were inhabited by other demographic groups.

If a European had made a film suggesting that superstition was universal among Africans, there would probably have been an outcry rather than the chorus of praise that greeted this film. And yet my experience of Africa, admittedly now three decades old, suggests that superstition of a kind that in a European would be deemed absurd is at the very least prevalent on the continent: and, if the film is anything to go by, such superstition has not decreased in the intervening period.

As I watched the film, I recalled my time in Tanzania. I was driving along an unpaved road in the bush, having given a lift to some Tanzanian soldiers, among whom was a captain. The road was in such a condition that I could not drive very fast. Some distance ahead in the road, I saw a chameleon crossing in a typically slow and ambivalent way, two rocking movements forward and one rocking movement back.

I like chameleons and find them infinitely fascinating creatures. They are both ugly and beautiful, and their ugliness and beauty are difficult to see at the same time, like one of those drawings that can either be seen as a candlestick or as two old crones, but not both at the same time. I stopped the vehicle and got out to capture the chameleon. I wanted to take it back with me so that I could watch it at my leisure. I picked it up and returned to the vehicle with it where, to my surprise, I saw the soldiers, including their captain, fleeing into the bush. They were evidently terrified, though chameleons are harmless to man, but they believed many strange things about them, the less bizarre among them, though still not true, being that their bite is highly venomous and that if they get in your hair, they can never be removed.

But their beliefs about them were deeper than this; for surely it was odd that people who had lived since time immemorial in the presence of chameleons should be less realistic about them than someone like me, with only the most passing of acquaintance with them. Then I imagined a Socratic dialogue as follows:

ME: Chameleons have been proved to be harmless.

THEM: But if touched or approached too near, chameleons bring sickness, accident, harm and death.

ME: That is all in your imagination.

THEM: No, this is our experience and that of our ancestors. If we touch or go too near a chameleon, we will fall ill, have an accident or die.

ME: If so, it will be either a coincidence or because of the workings of your imagination.

THEM: Whatever the reason, if we touch or go too near a chameleon, we will fall ill, have an accident or die.

And since everyone will fall ill, have an accident or die, too close an approach to chameleons can never be disproved as a cause, provided that there is no time-limitation placed on the ill-prognostication.

We do not have camps for witches, of course, but who would dare to say that we, as Shakespeare's love claimed to be, are made of truth?

I noticed with some amusement that this film was made with the financial aid of the Welsh Arts Council. In fact, most of the films that interested me on my cinematographic journey round the world turned out to have been made with state subsidies of one kind or another, and very few were purely commercial enterprises. Judging by the number of people who went to showings of most of those films, moreover, even the showings of them must have been subsidised from public funds. In effect, poor people in many different countries, including France, must in effect have been subsidising my pleasure. Whatever the morality of this, I was very glad they did, even being so kind as to reduce the price of my admission on account of my advanced age.

6

TASTE OF CEMENT, DIR. ZIAD KALTHOUM, LEBANON

Most people, I suspect, even those who follow the news assiduously, would find it difficult to provide a summary of the civil war in Syria. There are too many factions, there have been too many alliances and betrayals, too much foreign interference, too many cross-currents for a clear narrative to be possible. Moreover, in any such narrative, one wants there to be a good, or at least a better, side, so that there is the moral meaning so essential to narrative clarity. Who, when the war finally ends, and with whatever outcome, will dare say that virtue or progress has triumphed once and for all? And what state of future happiness could possible compensate or justify or make worthwhile all the suffering and death that the war has wrought?

Taste of Cement is a powerful documentary about refugee Syrian construction workers in Beirut, a city that has risen astonishingly — not for the first time — from its ashes. It films the lives of a group of such workers engaged on building a single skyscraper near Beirut's corniche. They work by day and after seven in the evening, at dusk, they retire to the underground bowels of their own skyscraper, for there is a permanent curfew on Syrian workers after that time. They are punished if they break it.

How the whirligig of time brings in its revenges! It is not so very long ago that Syrians came to the Lebanon as conquerors, occupiers and masters; now they are refugees and supplicants, fourth-rate citizens. There are said to be a million Syrians in the Lebanon, mostly working in construction. Perhaps the renaissance of Beirut actually needed the Syrian catastrophe, in a strange kind of dialectic, to provide it with an immense workforce glad to work for low wages in return for a degree of safety. Certainly, the most spectacular feats of urban construction in the Middle East in the last decades — Dubai, for example — have required (to say *have been based upon* would be to turn a necessary condition into a sufficient one) a ready fund of cheap labour. But let us avert our minds from these unpleasant thoughts and turn to something even worse.

Taste of Cement is not an ideological film. It does not seek for causes but rather presents the phenomena. Its subject is war and the pity of war. We see the Syrian workers as they work and then in their underground accommodation, where their entertainment, if such it can be called, consists mainly of following developments in Syria on their smartphones. (Telephonic communication still works, suggesting that it has now become the last thing to be destroyed, or the first thing to be restored, more important in effect than life itself.) There are no women among the Syrians and, assuming that the editing of the film — made, incidentally, with funds from the United Arab Emirates — has not been done deliberately to mislead, they speak little among themselves. The war, among other effects, has killed the desire, or perhaps even the capacity, for conversation.

Why are these men so silent among themselves, so atomised and asocial? Two hypotheses spring immediately to mind, not mutually exclusive or contradictory. The first is that their experiences have silenced them. If there are thoughts that lie too deep for tears, there are experiences that lie too deep for words, at least for anyone who is not a writer. My mother, who was a refugee, was a repository of experiences too deep for words, and she died without ever having communicated them; they died with her.

The second hypothesis is that they did not trust each other. It is possible that they were fleeing from different Syrian factions, that some of them were Alawites, others Christians, others Sunni, others Shia, all of them fleeing from the war of each against all. To have talked of their experiences, which would inevitably have ascribed the blame to one or other group, would have opened wounds, or rather poured salt into them, and reproduced the conflict from which they had fled. To concentrate on the work in hand — the construction of the skyscraper — was the only way to keep the peace and anaesthetise the mind even partially, at least for the moment.

The workers troop off, or rather up, to work every day, emerging from their subterranean lodgings, without any of the exuberance one would have expected elsewhere, but also with an impressive discipline that seems to have no exterior enforcement. Perhaps the fear of dismissal and forced return to Syria is sufficient to drill them into compliance. They are slaves without slave-drivers.

The work of construction itself surprised me, how much of it was performed by manual labour. When one ascends a finished skyscraper, say to the fiftieth floor, one does so without giving a second thought as to how it was constructed. Once it is there, one thinks of it almost as a natural phenomenon, a fact of nature like the Alps or the Mississippi. Are all skyscrapers built in the same labour-intensive way as in Beirut, or is it that they are built there in that fashion because the labour is available and cheaper than the machines that might otherwise do the work? I do not know and will probably never take the trouble to find out.

Irrelevant questions enter my mind as I watch films, sometimes with the persistence of an obsessional idea. In the film we see all the construction workers donning their hard-hats: and the question that ran through my mind is 'How many lives do such hats save on building sites such as this?' Do they really save lives, or are they more magical incantation than genuine precaution? If a crane hits you when you are fifty storeys up on a structure as yet without walls, will a hard-hat save you? Could hard-hats induce a false sense of safety, and thereby carelessness leading to accident and death? My mind is open on this question, as on so many others.

Also, and oddly, the men seem to be following no plan, to be working completely without orders of even foremen to tell them what to do, let alone architects or engineers. This must surely have been a deliberate effect created by editing.

Again, while one cannot but be impressed by the sheer scale of the building, at the technical brio necessary to construct it, one also knows perfectly well that when completed it will be completely banal in the sense that it will exactly resemble thousands of similar skyscrapers around the world. What kind of activity will go on in it, who or what is it for, what need does it answer that could not be supplied any other way? The workers, the tasters of cement, will never know: just as, high above the city below them, they will never participate in its obviously feverish prosperity. They are either high above the city or below it, but never of or in it.

It is when the sun goes down and they are forced underground that they become prey to their memories. One sees them watching newsreels of the war on their smartphones, some of the images filmed as reflections in their eyes. And then the film switches to sequences of the war itself, taken directly. They are among the most startling that I have ever seen. Many stay in the mind.

There is, for example, a sequence filmed from the balcony of a flat. A bomb or shell explodes at some distance, raising an immense, billowing cloud of cement dust that covers everything in a fawn-coloured obscurity; one hears the larger detritus rattling against the ironwork of the balcony and feels oneself preparing to choke.

Then there are the scenes of the desperate and chaotic efforts to release people trapped in concrete rubble after a bombardment, all carried out in half-light or in the narrow beams of torches. One almost feels one's leg trapped between blocks of concrete. The frantic selflessness of the searchers contrasts with the callous abstractness of the attack (by whomever launched, there is no indication of their identity).

Or yet again, the most dramatic of all, are the tank's eye views of the war. A video camera is attached to the turret of a tank as it moves, or crawls cautiously, through the former townscape now reduced to concrete rubble. There is no sign of an inhabitant, nor even that of a previous habitation: no crockery or curtains or furniture, not even a blade of grass. Everything has been reduced to anarchic piles of concrete and cement.

The tank is a mechanical, unfeeling monster, itself more or less the colour of the rubble it and other monsters like it have produced. But still it moves forward, in search of something to destroy. Oddly enough, the tank gives no impression of omnipotence, rather of vulnerability. Enemies with anti-tank weapons could be lurking anywhere in the ruins, despite the absence of signs of life. Sitting in the Parisian cinema, I felt vulnerable to attack at any moment. Would the sequences end with an attack on the tank? (We see no human agency at work in the tank.)

Having passed through scenes of total destruction, the tank gets a clear view of a relatively intact building. It appears, nevertheless, to be uninhabited and again gives no sign of life. At best it might be semi-habitable by those absolutely desperate for shelter. Why destroy it further? Better safe than sorry, however. The tank turret swivels in its direction and then fires. The remains of the building crumble and the tank immediately retreats, grinding in reverse. Oddly enough, though I was sixty-eight when I saw this, I had never realised before that a tank could reverse; I imagined them going only forwards. But as the tank reverses, its turret swivels constantly and almost nervously, as if scanning for enemies, its gun the antenna of an anxious iron insect. (Why do I say *as if* scanning for enemies? That was obviously what it was doing.)

The effectiveness of all these sequences is that there is no hint of purpose or reason behind the destruction. It is as if war were an end in itself. Never do we see anyone praying, let alone making a political speech. Not a slogan is to be seen in the film, and the only poster shown reminds the Syrian workers that breaking the 7pm curfew will be punished by law. The tasters of cement are never shown at prayer, nor do they appear to have any religious belief.

My contact with Syria and Syrians has been slight. I went to Syria for a few days in 1977 because the cheapest way to fly India was then with Syrian Arab Airlines. At Damascus airport, before being allowed on the plane, passengers had to identify their bags among all the luggage that was laid out on the apron. The theory then was that no one would board an aircraft knowing that there was a bomb on it. How naïve, almost quaint, this idea now seems to us!

Even then, of course, Syria was hardly a haven of peace. It was under the control of Assad *père*, whose regime was brutal and ruthless, trained terrorists and tortured opponents, was corrupt and horribly self-righteous at the same time, and so forth: but I loved Damascus as it then was. It had a great deal of charm and its life seemed to me civilised. One didn't hear the screams coming from the torture chambers, and though one knew that they were there, one could still enjoy the life of the city. I went to a performance of a famous Syrian female singer, whose performance was accompanied by the (frustrated?) howls of the male audience, all of which, except for myself, was Syrian. My only regret about having been to Syria was leaving it.

Not for the last time in my life, I discovered that a terrible regime was perfectly compatible with a country charming to visit, often more charming than countries with exemplary regimes. (Burma was another such.) I am not sure what to make of this observation. Political improvement can destroy charm. Does this charm weigh in the balance? Moreover, promised political improvement, while destroying charm, often brings deterioration. Again, I am unsure what to make of this.

At about this time, I had a Syrian colleague, a gentle soul who had come to England for training (as, later, did Assad *fils*). Gentle as he was, he had no doubt been witness to many things undreamed of in my philosophy up till then. We ate together, and I was friendly in a slightly condescending way — for I was callow. In truth, I expressed very little curiosity about his country or his experiences. I do not even know what his religion was, though I suspect he was a Christian. But in those far off days, his having been a Moslem would have been of no significance to me. One day he said something to me that showed me how far apart our cultures were. He said to me that we were brothers. In England, even brothers are not brothers.

Later, much later, I was asked to prepare a medical report on a Syrian refugee who had been totally incapacitated, or so he said, by the collision of a car that went into the back of his own car at five miles an hour. It was in Welwyn Garden City, where he lived. He had been in the Syrian army, where he had worked as a torturer. Unfortunately for him, he failed to give satisfaction in some way, and became an object of his previous type of endeavour, hence his status as a refugee. But it was the collision in Welwyn Garden City that reduced him to total invalidity.

Such is the story of Syria in my life, to which is now added *Taste of Cement*.

Postscript: This film was made while Lebanon was still booming and before its current collapse. Its boom, it turned out, was founded on a giant financial pyramid or Ponzi scheme, based on maintaining an artificial and unsustainable exchange rate between the Lebanese pound and the US dollar. It was also made before the giant explosion in Beirut's harbour.

Also, I should not omit to mention a book of photographs titled *Syria's War* by Narciso Contreras, published in 2014 by a company called War Photos Ltd., based in Dubrovnik, Croatia. This company specialises in high-quality and reasonably priced books of war photography, of current or recent conflicts. The books and their photographs are beautiful, compelling and terrible. Whether they risk aestheticizing war, I leave to others to decide. Suffice it to say that Narciso Contreras' book leaves one with thoughts and emotions not very dissimilar from those left by *Taste of Cement*.

7

MARIA BY CALLAS, DIR. TOM VOLF, GREECE

When I first went to the opera, singers seemed to be of three or four main types: the stately galleons, the battleships and the oil tankers, with occasional help from tugs. A considerable part of the staging involved either a type of naval battle or the avoidance of collision, including with the scenery, which might have been fatal, especially for the scenery. Maria Callas was known not to be of this ilk, and although some were critical of her voice, none doubted her dramatic power.

Although she died forty years ago, she still lives in the imagination as few other performers: but strangely enough I was ill informed about her life when I went to this film. My mind was full of rumour and prejudice about her, much of it unfavourable: she was the archetypical *prima donna*, capricious, egotistical and tempestuous, with a scandalous private life consequent upon those characteristics.

But as this film quickly persuaded me, nothing could have been further from the truth. She was a tragic figure who, despite the adulation (as well as the odium) she received, remained essentially a dignified, reserved, simple and honest person. It was a great pleasure to have my ideas, or rather prejudices, about her overturned: for at my age I am, and indeed much earlier I was, inclined to suffer from what a student friend of mine, who later became a distinguished professor of psychology, called a *hardening of the concepts*, a mental rigidity signalling the end of thought and even of rationality itself. A change of mind is rejuvenating.

Maria by Callas is a montage of newsreels, recordings of interviews and private films woven together to make a coherent story of her life. I had not expected to encounter someone so intelligent, articulate, sincere and (most surprising of all) modest. When she cancelled performances, something for which she was notorious, it was for a good reason and not for an attack of the vapours, as I had supposed. She wanted always to give of her best, her *quid pro quo* for her world fame. If the public adored her, she felt a genuine sense of obligation to it to be never anything less than at her best.

The film makes considerable use of a television interview she gave to David Frost, another person against whom I was prejudiced: but with her, at least, he was thoughtful and tactful, but at the same time searching in his questioning.

Maria Callas' unexpected absence of histrionics became clear to me when Frost asked her about her wartime experiences in Athens during the German occupation. Readers of Mark Mazower's brilliant account of that terrible time will understand and appreciate Callas' understatement that it was very hard: to which she added the Nietzschean thought that such experiences and hardship strengthen the character (provided, of course, that they are survived). She did not elaborate, and it would have been intrusive to have demanded that she did so. For myself, I was surprised that such an institution as the Athens Conservatoire — where she was studying — could have continued to function at such a time.

She was born in New York in 1924 to a somewhat vague father and a mother of ferocious ambition who wanted to make, and insisted on making, something exceptional of her daughter. Callas said that she would have much preferred to be a wife and mother, for that was her dream of a happy life (not a fashionable, or even avowable, dream these days); but it was not to be, her destiny was to be an opera singer, and she had to accept it. She never had children.

Written down like this, her statement might seem like an affectation on her part, to create an impression of modesty in a person avid for fame, but Callas says it so straightforwardly, so matter-of-factly, that one is completely persuaded that she is telling the simple truth. And since no unwanted career could have been more demanding than hers, albeit with its great rewards, one senses a life of tragedy and regret.

It was her mother who pushed her relentlessly. She took her back to Greece (from which she and her husband had emigrated) in 1937, and there insisted that Maria continue her musical education. By all accounts, she was a dedicated, serious and ferociously hard-working student, a perfectionist by nature. Her mother had at least chosen for her a career for which she was suited by her talents: and such are the contradictions inherent in human nature that Maria's own determination to succeed in something was not incompatible with a desire to be something else entirely. One learns with astonishment that it was in occupied Athens, in the midst of a most brutal occupation, that she made her operatic debut.

Her ascent to stardom was fairly rapid after the war and began in Italy. We see a collage of her successive triumphs together with the scandal caused by her cancellations, and her famous spat with Sir Rudolf Bing, the autocratic manager of the Metropolitan Opera in New York, justifying herself very convincingly. Bing wanted her to sing her roles opposite constantly changing tenors, and this (she said) was no way to mount productions of artistic integrity. Sir Rudolf in turn said that she was the most difficult singer with whom he had ever had to deal — because she was the most intelligent.

An important portion of the film, naturally enough, recounted her famous affair with Aristotle Onassis, the Greek shipping tycoon. My wife (who accompanied me) said that she could well see that Onassis was a very attractive man to women, but the fact is that he betrayed Callas in a shocking and heartless way. In the midst of his love affair with her, he went off and married the widow of President Kennedy, leaving her (Callas) to find out about the marriage by reading it in the newspapers. The letter that she wrote to him after finding out, read in the film, is almost unbearably moving, and reminded me of the letter to Tolstoy that the desperately ill Turgenev wrote on his deathbed. Callas' letter was loving, forbearing and unreproachful, precisely the opposite of what one might have expected of the hysteric I had once thought she was.

Tragically, Callas was a lost soul after Onassis' betrayal. She stopped singing and retired to her elegant flat in Paris. She continued to see Onassis, however, who admitted that in marrying Jacqueline Kennedy he had made 'a mistake'. This was not quite the word for it, perhaps, but in any case, their reconciliation came too late. Onassis was himself a dying man, and two years after his death, Callas died alone in her Parisian flat of a heart attack at the early age of fifty-three.

One leaves the cinema having undergone some kind of catharsis. The life of Callas was a long-unfolding tragedy. This glamorous woman, whose beauty far transcended the merely physical, whose talent allowed her to consort with the great ones of the world, and who must have made a considerable fortune, who was almost worshipped by her army of admirers (who admired her not without reason, unlike some of the more recent objects of mass adulation), was nevertheless deeply and profoundly, but privately, unhappy all her life. Her achievement was bought at incalculable cost, of which she gave only a glimpse in public; and in retrospect one understands that the dramatic quality of her singing and acting was directly the consequence of her inner life. She sang her life; she could almost have been Tosca herself, rather than merely portraying her.

I was deeply moved, and I think would have been just as moved if I had seen the film a second time. And yet, a little later, I began to worry a little about it. It had overturned my views entirely and now I was prepared to defend to the death Callas' reputation. I was prepared to be her posthumous knight in shining armour: but then the nagging question of whether my emotions had been manipulated by the film arose in my mind, and if they had, then what kind of person was I to be so quickly, so completely won over and manipulated? And if I was so easily manipulated, what of the great mass of mankind, what of democracy itself?

The narrative of the film was very simple, not to say

simplistic; talented but reluctant girl forced into a career she never wanted, has the love affair of her life, is betrayed, loses her reason to live, and dies alone of a heart attack. In the words of that great philosopher, William Clinton, we feel her pain, and feel good about ourselves for having done so.

But of course, there are omissions in the film, as no doubt there must be in the account of any life that is not as long as the life itself. We do not learn — we are not told — that Callas broke off all relations with her mother. Perhaps her mother was the demanding vixen portrayed, but even so it is hard to show such a break in a pleasing light. There is no mention of Callas' constant struggles with weight: she is always butterfly-beautiful, never larva or pupa. There is no mention of Guiseppe di Stefano, the Italian tenor with whom she is rumoured to have had a romantic liaison late in life (that is to say, late in the light of her early death). This might have spoiled the purity and emotional impact of the tragedy of her affair with Onassis. There is no mention of the possibility that her terminal decline might have been due to an illness, dermatomyositis, rather than to betrayed or unrequited love, which would certainly account for her death from heart attack, comparatively rare for a woman of her age. These complications, if admitted as part of the story, would have reduced its emotional impact somewhat, perhaps a great deal, and made its end, if not less painful, at least less pleasurable: for undiluted tragedy is like that bodily pain that it is a pleasure to exacerbate by pressing on the disordered part.

That I much prefer the version of Callas' life as relayed in this film does not make it true, but my preference will keep it alive in my memory for much longer.

One last small thing. In Callas' day, the opera was still a location of glamour and mystique. People still dressed up to go to the opera: no more. Now they dress down, if anything. At the Metropolitan recently, for example, I noticed that the audience seemed to be engaged on a competition of more-casually-dressed-than-thou. The men were unshaven, if not outright dirty: they wanted to look, or so it seemed, as if they had come directly to the opera from a building site or a warehouse. The women also made no particular effort, unless it was to demonstrate that they had made no particular effort. Only the bumpkins, as it were (like me), were so unsophisticated as to try to look smart and well-dressed.

What does this change signify, if anything? Certainly not the demise of a wealthy elite, which may dress down but has no intention of giving up its wealth. Perhaps there is a sufficient loss of belief in the legitimacy of economic differences for the elite to want to disguise itself as paupers to escape justified resentment. How can you hate a man for being rich when he is dressed in jeans and a t-shirt? By dressing badly, moreover, one proves that one is of the people.

Envoi: By strange coincidence, I read a book soon after seeing the film that presented an entirely different picture of Maria Callas. It was by Anthony Montague Browne, Winton Churchill's last private secretary. (I was writing a medical paper to refute the myth, now almost universally accepted, that Churchill suffered from severe depression, which clearly he did not.) After his retirement from politics, Churchill was invited several times by Onassis to cruise on his yacht in the Mediterranean. According to Browne, who was also aboard, Onassis took no particular interest in Callas until one day he suffered a slight head injury. He had dived into the shallow end of the swimming pool, struck his head on the bottom and suffered a concussion. Thereafter, his character changed. He became irritable but also took a great interest in Callas. Whether there is any truth to this story I cannot possibly say.

Browne certainly portrays Callas unflatteringly, however, as vain and egocentric. He recounts the following story of when Churchill, Callas and Onassis went ashore in Greece from the yacht:

> When we drove from the port of Neplion to the great Greek theatre of Epidaurus, the locals had erected a huge 'V' of flowers in the middle of the stage… Maria exclaimed 'Flowers for me! How kind!
>
> But why is it a V, Anthony?' I replied that it had undoubtedly been meant to be an M for Maria, but that they had not had time to finish it. Maria's reactive smile was [rapid]…

What is the truth about Callas? No wonder jesting Pilate did not stay for an answer when he had asked about the nature of truth in general.

8

LA JUSTE ROUTE (1945), DIR. FERENC TÖRÖK, HUNGARY

It is a common and ancient prejudice, which I struggle against unsuccessfully in my own mind, that one's true character emerges only in the most extreme circumstances, when put to the most severe test. That test must be one of great misfortune, though in fact great good fortune is as much a test of character as great ill-fortune, albeit of a somewhat more subtle nature. According to the view that great ill-fortune alone tells us what a man 'really' is, all that leads up to that ill-fortune is at best a rehearsal for it, at worse an irrelevance. No one is good until he has shown himself good in adversity.

Those of us who missed the war by a few years — the Second World War, that is — naturally ask ourselves what we would have done in it, and even how we should have behaved under occupation by the Nazis. The French author, Pierre Bayard, wrote a book, *Aurais-je été resistant ou bourreau?* — Would I Have Been in the Resistance or an Executioner? — to which he gave the modest and realistic answer that he would probably have been neither.

In this film, two Orthodox Jewish survivors of the Holocaust, one of them an elderly man and the other young, arrive not long after the end of the war in a village on the Hungarian plain, in the midst of flat farmland. The villagers, particularly the secretary of the local council, have bad consciences: not only have they taken the property of the Jews who used to live in the village, and now use it as their own, but some of them actually 'denounced' the Jews to the authorities in the full knowledge and understanding that they would be deported and killed. They did so, moreover, before there was any real coercion to do so, the implication being that they did it eagerly, joyfully. In the course of the film it becomes clear that the local priest, suspiciously portly and well fed in the post-war circumstances, was complicit in this. The owners of the Jews' property, to which they now have title according to the legal form of the time, fear that the two Jews, who arrive completely unheralded at the nearby station, and who were previously unknown in the village, have come to reclaim the property on behalf of its former owners, the Pollaki family, of whom they are the descendants.

The photography in the film is superb. I have never quite understood why, but undramatic landscape makes for the best or most evocative painting. You might think that the most splendid scenes would evoke the strongest or most deeply emotional of responses, but this is not so. Dramatic landscape, when represented, easily becomes kitsch, and grandeur is not necessarily sublimity.

The shot of a line of trees in a flat landscape, seen through the stubble of a harvested field, is memorable, though also in a sense banal, and all the more memorable for being in black and white rather than in colour, which would have been a distraction. Again, in a way that I cannot fully analyse, the monochromaticism adds, if not to the realism, at least to the intensity of the scene. The 1940s were an era best expressed in monochrome, although their skies must have been just as blue and the grass just as green as in subsequent decades.

Until they were denounced and deported, the Jewish family owned the village store and pharmacy. They are now owned by the secretary of the council, who has duly stamped and sealed (but morally illegitimate) title to them. In normal times he would have nothing to worry about, but the aftermath of a genocide is not a normal time, nor is (the as yet incomplete) Soviet domination reassuring to property-owners. Title is not worth the parchment it is written on.

The threat of the installation of a regime that does not recognise private property is signified by the passage through the village of a jeep with Soviet soldiers in it, in such a manner as to indicate where power in Hungary now really lies or will soon lie. But for the moment the villagers are obsessed still with property, as if its possession could be solidly established.

The two Orthodox Jews decide, on arrival at the station, to walk to the village a few kilometres away. They do so, erect, solemn and silent, looking neither to the left nor the right, behind a horse cart that they have hired and on which are carried two metal trunks. The news of their arrival precedes them and throws the village into a panic. What do the tin trunks contain? The villagers surmise that they contain perfumes and other beauty products for sale in the pharmacy once they have taken it back into possession as legatees of the deported former owners.

But the two Jews continue through the village to the village cemetery. There they order the owner of the cart that they have hired to dig a kind of grave. When they have done so, the two Jews bury the contents of their trunks — prayer shawls, the clothes of the former owners of the pharmacy and the small shoes of their children — in the grave. Having done this, they return on foot to the station.

Here I must admit that I found it implausible, and perhaps a little sentimental, that any of the belongings of the exterminated Jewish villagers could have been identified in this way and then buried. Surely their belongings would simply have been piled up and disposed of collectively, without identification? If the belongings were not literally those of the deported villagers, but only symbolically so, would anyone have gone to the trouble that the two Orthodox Jews have gone to?

As soon as it becomes clear to the villagers that the two visitors have not come to reclaim anything, their attitude changes. Their relief is palpable. They shake hands with the Jews and express condolences for their losses. Their new unctuous politeness is, if anything, even more disgusting than their initial hostility and mistrust; they think they have been let off the hook.

But they haven't been. One of them, a fat peasant, has long had an uneasy conscience and, drinking very heavily, hangs himself. (The Hungarians, by the way, have long had the highest suicide rate in the world, at least since any statistics existed.) The council secretary's son, about to be married to a village girl who is herself really in love with the village communist who anticipates the Russian takeover with glee, and who regards his father both as unscrupulous and very oppressive, decides to leave the village for Budapest. The village girl who was to be his bride burns down the pharmacy: the whirligig of time has brought in its revenges.

With the slight exception, perhaps, of the burial scene, the film is without sentimentality. For its duration, one feels oneself the living observer of that village on the Hungarian plain in 1945, during the brief interregnum before the communists take over. The cross-currents of greed, guilt and the attempted return to normal existence as if nothing had happened or changed, are evident through the film. But life can never return to the *status quo ante*, not for these people.

Throughout the film, I thought of Jean Hatzfeldt's magnificent series of books about the Rwandan genocide, in which he interviews the survivors, the perpetrators, and both who have subsequently to live together in the aftermath. The parallels are not exact, of course, but suggestive in the Hungary of the film, the villagers did not commit the killings themselves, as villagers did in Rwanda, but rather were actively complicit in them; nor, in the case of these villagers, were the numbers comparable (though they were for the whole of the country). And yet the shamelessness and even joy with which the material goods of the victims were appropriated were eerily similar and very disturbing. Envy and greed very soon overcame all normal ethical inhibition. In 'normal' times, the successful minority group, Jew or Tutsi, might be tolerated though disliked, principally because of its success; but as soon as genocide was sanctioned or promoted as a patriotic duty, material avidity overcame the most elementary decency. Here is Alphonse, speaking about what happened after a day's slaughter of the Tutsi:

The first evening, on returning from the massacre in the church, the reception was well-organised by the leaders…. Shots were fired in the air, whistles were blown and musical instruments played. The children pushed the cows rounded up that day into the middle [of the football field]. The Burgomaster Bernard offered the forty fattest to the *interahamwe* [*those who work together*, i.e. killers with machetes]…

This was to encourage the rest of the villagers to follow suit, for if guilt is spread widely enough, it ceases to exist.

If by numbers the obvious brutality of Rwandan villagers was worse than that of the Hungarian, in one respect, perhaps, the Hungarian was worse. In Rwanda a situation was created in which it was genuinely dangerous for the Hutu peasants not to participate: they would be killed themselves if they did not. But in Hungary, an element of choice remained. One of the villagers, the council secretary's wife, was entrusted with the money of the deported Jews and instead of spending it, she hid it against their return. She was better than her husband.

Thus, even in an extreme situation there is often better and worse behaviour, between joyful and reluctant complicity, between self-advancement and self-preservation.

9

ENQUÊTE AU PARADIS, DIR. MERZAK ALLOUACHE, ALGERIA

Heaven seems to me the most slippery of concepts and no visual depiction of it ever as vivid as depictions of Hell. We can all easily imagine a life of eternal pain, surviving forever, say, in bubbling cauldrons while being poked in the sides by devils with tridents, but eternal bliss is much harder to imagine. Happiness is more dependent on the possibility and proximity of its opposite than is misery; and bliss, in our experience, is necessarily a short-lived state. There is no bliss without limitation of time and without intimate knowledge of other states of mind, which is why Keats tells us:

Ay, in the very temple of delight
Veil'd Melancholy has her sovran shrine…

And yet it seems that the prospect of Paradise is very real to those young Moslem fanatics who blow themselves up (and more importantly others) in the belief that they will thereby bypass the inevitable disappointments, inconveniences and sufferings of this, our earthly existence, and attain the glories of Heaven in the shortest way possible. They are simultaneously optimistic and pessimistic: the latter about the prospects and possibilities of life, and the former about the likelihood both of the existence of Heaven and of going straight there, like first-class passengers avoiding the frustrations of modern airports, boarding the plane before everyone else.

But what do they expect of heaven? In this film, a young Algerian woman journalist, very secularised, and her equally secularised male associate, try to find out what Algerians think heaven will be like.[2] Also a film in black and white, they interview numerous people in various situations and walks of life.

There are, of course, inherent difficulties in knowing what to make in an enquiry of this kind: its value is entirely dependent on the intellectual honesty of those who conduct it, for it is surely possible in a large population to find whatever the enquirers set out to find. The viewer is at the mercy of the film-maker and the editing process, and because of the power of a medium that purports to present immediate and unvarnished reality before the viewer's very eyes, the latter is inclined to believe that what he is seeing is precisely that, reality itself. Even the film-maker may not be aware of the problem, any more than a patient who recovers from an illness after having taken some pills is often not aware of the fact that his recovery does not prove that the pills worked. But if

---

[2] *Enquête au paradis* is a hybrid film. The journalist and her associate are actors playing young journalists, but the interviewees are not actors.

seriously dishonest, the film-maker can so edit that people can be made to say something very different from what they meant. This has happened to me sufficiently often that I am reluctant to be interviewed other than live. Of course, a social phenomenon such as a belief in paradise does not have to be statistically average to be of social importance. Those who attacked the World Trade Center in New York were clearly not statistically representative of any large group, but they were not without importance. So even if the film's interviewees were highly selected and therefore not representative, one could not conclude that the film was itself therefore of no significance.

It begins by showing a recording of a Saudi Wahhabi preacher, the very caricature of the type (white robes and shawl over his head, and an unruly beard wagging with vigorous anger and self-righteousness), preaching a sermon about Paradise. It is, in a sense, shockingly vulgar, stupid, materialistic, funny and kitsch: this man who probably believes that music and laughter are haram (forbidden), that dogs are ritually unclean and must never be kept as pets, that adulterers should be stoned and apostates and homosexuals killed, that women displaying an inch of flesh are prostitutes and should be whipped, as should those failing to attend Friday prayers, also imagines paradise as an eternal hybrid between Palm Beach and the Moulin Rouge, with men titillated eternally by seventy-two undeflowerable virgins (whose opinion on this or on any other subject is not solicited), where every orgasm lasts a thousand years and every meal is of the finest imaginable ingredients. In short, it is the paradise dreamed of by frustrated and dirty old men.[3]

As the preacher's imagination grows ever more fevered, as his beard wags ever more venomously or salaciously, the small audience in the cinema, mainly women, laughed: and indeed it was ludicrous, as Hitler's speeches now appear ludicrous. How could any grown man of normal intelligence believe the things he believed, apparently as indubitable and completely beyond question? Perhaps his very vehemence was a sign of inner doubt rather than of certainty, as if the person he was most trying to persuade were himself. Of course, the belief that, where human conduct is concerned, appearances are often the opposite of the truth, that certainty is doubt, kindness is sadism, and so forth, is intuitive and itself open to doubt, but the fact that mullahs who extol martyrdom rarely volunteer for it themselves suggests to me that they are less than frank about their own motives.

Hypocrite or sincere, it is wrong merely to laugh at such a preacher: for the fact is that, whether or not sincere, some young people will take him seriously, as if what he said were true. A suicide bomber is sincere, which suggests that sincerity is not by itself a virtue.

The protagonist of the film, the woman journalist, seems to have no difficulty in finding young men who believe in the seventy-two virgin type paradise, even superficially westernised young men in an internet café, dressed in a

---

[3] He promises (male) entrants to Paradise brunettes with superb breasts and thighs, perpetually virgin, whose softness requires no Vaseline or Nivea. He says this in so many words.

fashion that would not be out of place in any western city. The surely intended implication is that these young men, if they believe in the reality of such a paradise, are but a short step from terrorism, or at least vulnerable to its siren-song. The young men are neither stupid (in the sense of lacking native intelligence) nor illiterate. They are probably no worse educated than many in Britain or America, nor do they give the impression of being nasty or unpleasant. On the contrary, they have an unselfconscious charm not universal among western youth. Moreover, they seem bright and optimistic in the best manner of young people who have all before them. According to the interviewed owner of the internet café, the most common subject of their internet searches is how to obtain a visa for France.

And yet, when it comes to the subject of paradise, they display what seems to me to be a primitive credulity. What the Koran promises must be true because the Koran is the Koran. That the Koran, however interpreted, might be wrong, is simply not a possibility for them. It is as if their minds had been implanted from the earliest age by a kind of ineradicable software virus, rendering them incapable of examining what most people not so inoculated would consider an absurd and primitive dogma. They reminded me of those paranoid persons who are perfectly rational (insofar as anyone is perfectly rational) on all subjects until you touch upon the one subject about which they are deluded. The nature of a delusion is, of course, that it is impervious to reason, argument or evidence, and as far as these young men are concerned, if religious authority says seventy-two virgins, seventy-two virgins it must be.

The journalist interviews Boualem Sansal, an Algerian civil servant turned successful writer (successful in France that is, not in Algeria, where his books have been banned). Sansal could be a Parisian intellectual: he looks and sounds entirely the part. His book-lined apartment could be on the Left Bank, entirely French in style, though I think it was in Algiers. He speaks the most beautiful and limpid French, clear and lucid. This disposed me in his favour, all the more so as his analysis so nearly coincided with my own.

It was as if, he said, Algerians had two sides of the brain, as indeed did people of other Islamic countries. With one half of their brain, they thought perfectly normally. They analysed problems in rational fashion. They could be engineers, doctors, pharmacists or whatever, and appear no different from engineers, doctors or pharmacists anywhere else. Their religion, however, was in the other half of their brain, from which completely irrational notions emanated. They had no way of connecting these two types of cerebration and therefore lived in a permanent state of splitting. They were fully aware of this but could do nothing about it. However, until they resolved the problem the country could not progress. M. Sansal was very persuasive, at least to me.

Of course, it might be said that religious people everywhere are split in this fashion. The great Isaac Newton was possessed of some very strange and to us absurd ideas that seemed more important to him than all his researches. But there is, at least as things now are, a particular problem with Islam and the Islamic world, namely the more extensive claims of Islam over every part and aspect of human existence. It is inherently caesaropapist in ambition, but with no means of resolving who is pope. Moslems seem to be left with a choice between hypocrisy and fanaticism.

Sansal came across as a very impressive man, and as soon as I could, I ordered some of his books. I am ashamed to say that I did not know of him before. The cinema can extend your mind.

Although I was in fundamental sympathy with the obviously secular outlook of the protagonist, and could not but feel something like contempt for the interviewees' belief in paradise, or rather for what they thought they would find there, I could not but find also the protagonist rather smug in her sense of moral and intellectual superiority over those whom she interviewed. She was as certain in her own way that she was right as was the Saudi preacher, and such certainty is rarely attractive.

The film is long and self-indulgent and with several redundant passages. It was almost as if the makers attributed significance to every thought or utterance of the protagonist. In one part of the film she goes to the south of the country (far less westernised than Algiers, of course), to the town of Timmoun. All the women there are dressed in full garb, revealing nothing. The journalist, still dressed in western fashion, approaches them to canvass their conception of heaven. All too predictably, they refuse to speak to her, almost certainly putting her down as a loose woman (at best). They walk past her as if they have neither seen nor heard her. But if she had been really interested in what they thought, she would surely have disguised herself. Even then, they might not have spoken to her (presumably there would still have been men holding microphones and video cameras, and Islam enjoins women not to speak before strange men, as I was told as a child not to speak to strangers). She is therefore not so much enquiring what they think as demonstrating her modernity, the gulf between her and them, for all to see.

Algeria is shown as a country in which people from an early age fear to speak their minds. The protagonist attempts to interview pupils emerging from a lycée in Algiers. They resemble their French counterparts very closely, but they refuse to speak to her, and not from shyness or modesty. But they are nevertheless members of the westernised elite.

An Algerian psychiatrist interviewed about them says the Algerian schools are not producing citizens but inquisitors. Are we not going in the same direction?

10

CENTAURE, DIR. AKTAN ARYM KUBAT, KYRGYZSTAN

A few days after I saw this film from Kyrgyzstan (which used to be known as Kirgizstan or even Kirgizia), I had lunch with a charming Russian woman who told me, to my great surprise, that in Soviet days Kirgiz films were known for their high quality.

I was particularly anxious to see the film because I had once been to Kyrgyzstan, the small, once Soviet, Central Asian republic. I went in the days immediately following the break-up of the Soviet Union when I was the member of a busybody group that went round monitoring elections behind the former Iron Curtain for their freeness and fairness, not qualities to be taken for granted in countries in which leaders had previously been elected with 99.6 per cent of the votes cast. My motives were essentially frivolous, because I didn't really believe in the possibility of freeness and fairness in former Soviet Central Asian republics (or in Albania or Georgia for that matter, another among several of the countries whose elections we monitored). I was like the boy in the poem by Keats:

There was a naughty boy,
And a naughty boy was he.
He ran away to Scotland,
The people for to see.

The idea of there being more than one candidate was clearly a strange and disturbing innovation. The Organization for Security and Co-operation in Europe (O.S.C.E.) also sent observers, and the strange thing was that they always observed the mirror-image of what we observed. The more fraudulent the elections, the more the O.S.C.E. praised them for their rectitude; conversely, the more honestly they were conducted (relatively speaking, of course), the more fraudulent the O.S.C.E. declared them to have been. We decided, with the certitude of the paranoid, that the O.S.C.E. had a hidden agenda: for reasons best known to its masters, it wanted certain candidates to win and others to lose, come what may. Its reports had nothing to do with what had actually happened and everything to do with its political agenda.

Bishkek, the capital of Kirghizstan, as it was then still called, was a typical product of Soviet urban planning and architecture: grandiose, grey, tasteless, windswept and empty, a completely alien concrete wasteland seemingly arbitrarily imposed on the landscape of steppe and mountain, with kitsch brutalist monuments to people like Mikhail Frunze. Frunze was a successful military leader, born in the city, who was probably assassinated on Stalin's orders in 1925 because of his charisma and popularity, and was posthumously rewarded (by Stalin) by having the military academy and the city in which he was born named after him[4]. The main hotel in Bishkek was still in the Intourist style, with prostitutes in the lobby and Cuban entertainers in the bar-cabaret. Ever since then I have wondered — intermittently — what it must have been like to have been a Cuban singer or dancer in post-Soviet Kyrgyzstan. The hotel was empty, but the show had to go on before an audience of eight or ten in a large, cold and cavernous auditorium. To keep up enthusiasm and gaiety in such circumstances took an heroic effort, but change was coming: a casino had been added.

The theme of the film was the loss under the new dispensation of the country's soul. To Soviet-style modernization had been added rampant, brazen, crude and grasping materialism, the main symbol of Kirghiz culture, the horse, having become a mere commodity and plaything of the rich rather than the spiritual symbol and guarantor of Kirghiz liberty.

In *Centaure*, the protagonist, played by the director, is a former cinema projector and horse-thief called Centaur. He is married to a deaf-mute by whom he has a son who is mute but not deaf. He, Centaur, lives in a village and has a cousin who is the local businessman made good (by what means, or in what business, is not made clear, but virtually by definition in post-Soviet conditions shady). Horses are a hobby for the rich

---

[4] Frunze suffered from peptic ulceration and underwent an operation from which he never woke. Suspicion attaches to Stalin because he advised and even insisted upon the operation, which the doctors did not.

cousin as well as a business, inasmuch as he enters his horses for races on which a lot of money is staked.

One day Centaur steals one of his cousin's prize horses worth fifty thousand dollars. He does so not to make money or sell it, but so that he can ride it freely on the steppe, without saddle, reins or spurs, feeling the wind in his face and running through his hair. In his opinion, horses are not a commodity but a means to reject the constraints of a world in which money is the measure of all things. He has something of the urban joy-rider in him, who takes cars for pleasure rather than for profit and to release himself for a time from his otherwise grey, hopeless or sordid daily life.

When his cousin discovers that his horse has been stolen, he assumes that it was taken by a well-known, local, small-time thief rather than his cousin and, symbolically of the power of the rich in such a society, he captures the man he suspects and beats him severely in an attempt to obtain from him the whereabouts of his horse. The small-time thief cannot give him this, of course, and a little while later the horse mysteriously reappears in his stable.

The true thief comes to light; he is caught and tried in the village court in which everyone in the village has his say as to how the thief should be punished. (The swiftness and flexibility of the trial makes our legal system seem slow, cumbersome, inefficient and rigid by comparison, and one falls prey for a moment to the illusion that such justice is superior to our own, forgetting how arbitrary, unfair and prejudiced swift justice would be in a society as complex as ours.) The thief's cousin has the most to say. He has listened to Centaur's self-justification, namely that the world, or at least Kyrgyzstan, has lost its enchantment, that the Kirghiz were once a race of noble warriors who lived free on the steppe, but look at them now, etc. etc., corrupted by the desire to accumulate possessions, soulless and depraved. This is an indictment that his cousin knows to be true and at least partly accepts, and so he proposes as punishment for Centaur that he make the pilgrimage to Mecca — the Kirghiz are Moslems, nominally at least — with a small group of rigorous Moslems who have suddenly appeared in the village as missionaries for a closer observance of the faith. This more rigorous faith is another way of confronting the spiritual loss that modernization and its rampant materialism have brought in their wake.

For a short time, Centaur becomes a pious Moslem. He has his head shaved, and he now wears a costume that singles him out as a pious Moslem, but this phase does not last long. He goes to the village hall in which he once used to project films, but which the Moslem missionaries have succeeded in turning into a mosque. He joins them in his prayers but is soon revolted, being a lover of freedom, by the mindless, repetitive, mechanical, militarily coordinated nature of the prayers. He creeps away from his fellow-congregants and ascends to the gallery from which films were once projected and where the old projector remains disused. In the middle of the prayers of those whom he has left below, he begins to project an old film, not coincidentally of a woman joyfully riding a horse. The anti-Islamic symbolism could hardly be more explicit.

He is then tried for a second time in the village. The local population is very far from being fanatically religious, yet the hold of Islam on them is sufficiently strong, or they dare not admit otherwise, that they cannot let this insult go unpunished. Centaur is expelled from the village.

He duly leaves the village, but as he does so he finds a herd of horses which he releases into freedom. As the horses gallop away, the owners of the herd see him and shoot him dead.

There is a sub-plot in the film concerning Centaur's relationship with his deaf-mute wife. She is a beautiful, sweet-natured woman who loves Centaur deeply. Unfortunately, a village gossip informs her (in writing) that Centaur has been seeing another woman in the village. Indeed, he has, but innocently; and the village gossip, who disguises her malice by pretending a friendship towards Centaur's wife, poisons her mind so that the touchingly successful marriage has broken up by the time of Centaur's expulsion from the village. This is movingly portrayed, and one feels anger towards the village gossip who, from motiveless malignity such as can be found everywhere in the world, destroys the happiness of the couple and their son.

A Russian friend of mind told me that the Soviets had made some very good films but that most of them were marred by sudden unaccountable lapses of taste. This film was not Soviet, to be sure, and the language throughout was Kirghiz, not Russian; but the Soviet influence was patent, down to the lapse of taste.[5]

The lapse of taste came when Centaur was shown riding his horse freely without reins or saddle, all filmed in slow

---

[5] I do not, of course, mean that lapses of taste are unique to Soviet or Soviet-influenced films. Indeed, there are some films that lapse *into*, rather than *from*, good taste.

motion. Worse still, Centaur sat bolt upright on the horse, his arms stretched outwards and upwards, the sky above blue and the mountains in the background. This was kitsch of rare purity, all the more jarring because the film was otherwise without sentimentality.

The theme is the large one of loss brought about by change, even change that one might consider progress. I think anyone of sensibility — certainly no one who has lived long enough to look back from a certain distance on his life — has not experienced a sense of loss in change, even when that change is largely for the better. Indeed, to regret nothing about the past, to feel no nostalgia at all for it, is a pitiful condition insofar as it implies a wholly wretched or impoverished prior existence. Though nostalgia is often derided as worthless or destructive or even despicable, he who bounds into the future without so much as a painful look back is much to be feared, a fifth horseman of the Apocalypse who knows not what he does.

The idea that we in the present have lost our soul because of our materialism is a recurrent one, and also beguiling. Like so many truths of the human condition, this one is partial and easily lends itself to humbug. I caught myself thinking, as I saw Kyrgyzstan's open spaces, how wonderful it would be to live free of the dross of modern civilization. Then I remembered my tour to the Highlands of Scotland fifty years earlier.

I was in a bar in Skye (there was no bridge from the mainland in those days). It was summer. There were a couple of weather-beaten islanders in the bar at the time. I pronounced a dithyramb to the beauty of the landscape, the simplicity of the life, and so forth, and how wonderful it must be to live there.

'You should be here in fucken February,' said one of the men in the bar.

No wind had ever been more comprehensively or swiftly taken out of anyone's sails. Ever since, whenever I have been tempted to indulge in dithyrambs about the simple life (in Kirghizstan, for example), I remind myself that I should be there in fucken February.

11

DOKHTAR, DIR. REZA MIRKARIMI, IRAN

It is half a century since I went to Iran for the first and only time in my life (unless you count the return overland journey from India as a second time, when I was briefly held in quarantine because there had been an outbreak of cholera in Afghanistan through which I had just passed). His Imperial Majesty the Shahanshah was still on the throne. The times were not propitious for imperial majesties (as far as I know, only one remains), but I had no intuition or intimation that the Shah of Shahs was not to reign for the rest of his life. And even if I had imagined an end to the Shah's regime, I should have imagined it brought about by the communists, the Tudeh party, rather than by the Islamists. In Teheran, or at least in the part of Teheran that I saw, the Shah's White Revolution seemed to have taken deep root, as had secularism in general. The doctrine of the time was that secularization was an irreversible process, a one-way street, in the way that an omelette cannot be returned to the condition of eggs. This turned out to be a mistake: if I may change the metaphor, I mistook the veneer for the wood.

But how religious is Iran really? Might we not be making

the same mistake, only in reverse? Without knowing a society in its intimate details (and perhaps not even then), who can say what is really going on in it? The greatest experts, who for years have studied nothing else, may be taken completely by surprise by the turn of events. This is not a plea for ignorance but for modesty. There is a tendency to see a film and think one knows a country.

Dokhtar is a family drama set initially in Abadan, the southern oil port now somewhat dilapidated after years of economic sanctions against Iran. Ahmad, the hero of the film (if that is quite the word for him), is the engineer of the port in charge of maintenance. He tries to protect his workers from the unreasonable demands of the more senior management, but at home *he* is the senior management with unreasonable demands, in fact he is the absolute dictator.

His youngest daughter (who has been to university) wants to take a day trip to Teheran to attend a farewell party for one of her friends who is leaving Iran for Canada. The party is an innocent one for girls only and the daughter promises to return the same day. But Ahmad — fat, humourless and singularly unattractive — refuses his permission for two reasons: first, it is the day of her sister's engagement party, and second, Ahmad does not trust her. The request alone is enough to arouse his suspicions, for if a daughter of his should be seen in the company of a young man without permission, the honour of the whole family, especially that of the paterfamilias himself, would be impugned.

The daughter defies him and goes on her day trip anyway. Unfortunately, the return flight is cancelled owing to heavy pollution in Abadan, so that she cannot return as she had planned. When she fails to return, Ahmad immediately sets out in his car to retrieve her from Teheran, though the journey in the night is very long and tedious.

Why does he think it so important that his daughter should not stay overnight in Teheran at the home of a friend? She is, after all, in her early twenties, not a child in need of constant protection. Is it anxiety, then, that she might come to some terrible harm? Hardly. Is it that she might be consorting with a young man? Yes, but that only pushes the question one stage back: why is it so important that she should not consort with a young man? As the film makes clear, she is not exactly a slut. Even her relations with a young man, were she to have any, would more likely be innocent than torrid. But for Ahmad, her failure to return is hardly any worse than her decision to defy him and go in the first place. It is his authority that has been challenged, his dictatorship. Her departure alone is a humiliation for him, and he fears that anyone who comes to know of it would scorn him. His honour is at stake.

When he reaches Teheran, he finds her at the home of her friend's family and leads her away. He is silent but menacing. As he drives away, he says not a word. His daughter begs him to speak, but he maintains an infuriated silence. She confesses her sin and acknowledges that she has behaved very badly. Distracted by her as she is pleading with him, he knocks over a motor cyclist. He strikes his daughter in frustration, and then gets out of the car to attend to, or rather have an argument with, the motorcyclist (the accident was none of the motorcyclist's fault, but that does not prevent him from being aggressive towards him). Fortunately, the motorcyclist is not injured, but when Ahmad returns to the car, his daughter has fled.

We see then that though he is an unattractive man, unreflectively authoritarian, bullying and physically almost repellent (he is one of those fat men who has not yet gone entirely to seed, so that he remains very strong), Ahmad has real love for his daughter, though he never expresses it by tenderness. It is as though expressing his love in that way would be an admission of weakness or vulnerability, a possible weapon that could be used against him. In the same way, his daughter is not merely fearful of him physically, but of losing his love. She, too, loves him.

She has fled to the home of her aunt, her father's sister. This sister has herself rejected Ahmad's authority by marrying a man of whom he disapproved (he having been the head of the family at the time). Unfortunately, the man she chose to marry turned out to be unsuitable and brought her nothing but unhappiness. The escape from tyranny does not always result in lasting joy.

Learning that his daughter is living with his sister in Teheran, Ahmad comes to stay in order to persuade her to come home. Gradually, but very slowly, he unfreezes. Once or twice he even smiles. He helps cook a meal, for example by gutting and scaling a fish, his very presence in the kitchen being evidence of a change of heart. It is while he is in the kitchen one day that his sister launches into a diatribe against him: how he always thinks he is right, how he has always unquestioningly believed in his own authority and that he had the right to order others about, tell them what to do and how to live their lives, and so forth. Of course, he does not accept what she says and answers back; nevertheless, the diatribe has an effect. The last scene shows him on the flat roof of the house, obviously in reflective mood. We still may not like him very much, but we cannot think of him as an irredeemably bad man.

Ahmad is conservative but does not seem excessively religious. True, he asks his sister for a prayer rug and the direction of Mecca in which, of course, he should pray. But we do not see him actually praying, nor does he make any religious references or cite any religious reasons for his conduct as paterfamilias. Iran, at least as depicted here, does not appear a religious country (albeit that all the women wear obligatory headscarves). Rather, Iran appears as a middle-income country on the path of secular economic development — well on the way, in fact, to resuming the Shah's White Revolution.

Thus, Ahmad is authoritarian not because he lives in a country in which every father is a paterfamilias, but as a matter of personal choice. The fathers of his daughter's friends are not like him but much more liberal. If his conduct was once universal, it is so no longer. His problem, if such it be considered, is a personal and psychological rather than a social one.

How did his authoritarianism arise and by what is it maintained? It is partly a cultural hangover, of course, and the film shows that the transition to modernity is not made by a single leap, not even in a single human heart, let alone in an entire society. But Ahmad's desire to impose his authority is hardly unique to him or to Iran. If the inherent human propensity to seek power and authority were distributed normally, on a bell-shaped curve, such that at one end of the distribution were people inclined to it by nature, and at the other end disinclined to it, a change in the culture of a society might increase or reduce the expression of power in personal relationships. Ahmad is a man inclined to authoritarianism in a society in which it is in decline.

When I practised as a doctor, there was a society within a society in which extreme familial authoritarianism, much greater than that of Ahmad, was common. I speak of the Pakistani Moslem immigrants. The young women of this society were sometimes kept apart, having often been prevented illegally from attending school without intervention by the authorities. They would be forced to marry their first cousin back 'home', a home which they had never seen and a cousin on whom they had never previously clapped eyes. They all know of girls who had refused to marry their first cousins and suffered the direst consequences.

I came to know the story by heart. They were told that they were going on holiday to Pakistan. They were given their passports as they went through passport control at both ends of the journey, but the father would at all other times take control of them. Once back 'home' they were told they were to be married, and if they refused, they were imprisoned or beaten into obedience.

'O sweet my mother, cast me not away,' pleads Juliet when she appeals to her mother to intercede with her father who is trying to force a marriage on her. When the young women of Pakistani descent pleaded with their mothers in exactly the same way as Shakespeare recounts, they (the mothers) would often fall to the ground, claiming to have had a heart attack that would only worsen if the daughter did not accede to the fathers' demands. When I asked my young Pakistani patients whether their mothers had ever behaved in this way, they were astonished: how did I know? And having previously been tearful, they would start to laugh.

Part of the tragedy of these girls forced to marry against their will was that they loved the father who was forcing them, as Ahmad's daughter loves her father. Moreover, the fathers genuinely thought that they were acting in the best interests of their daughters whom in turn they loved. But family honour was also at stake. They had promised the hand of their daughter, and honour required that the promise was kept.

Try as I might to empathise or sympathise with this sense of honour, such that a man might sacrifice his own daughter to it, I found that I could not. There are limits to sympathy. I understood Ahmad from the outside, but I could not imagine what it would be like to *feel* like him. His scale of values was mysterious to me because of my very different upbringing. I could imagine what it was like to be Richard II or Richard III, or even Iago, but not Ahmad. Perhaps it was sufficient to know Ahmad from the outside and to know that he was capable of change.

12

CANDELARIA, DIR. JHONNY HENDRIX HINESTROZA, CUBA

It so happened that on the day on which I decided to see this film, I read a review in *Le Monde des livres* (the books pages of the French newspaper supposedly of record, though no newspaper really serves that function these days) of *La Lutte*, a book by the sociologist and anthropologist, Vincent Bloch, on the situation in Cuba after the implosion or dissolution of the Soviet Union and the end of aid to the communist island fortress:

> For those who, after a visit to Cuba, return seduced by the warmth of the people and in ecstasies over the free education and healthcare, I cannot recommend too highly reading the 200 central pages of this new book... It is a Balzacian story, meticulous and engrossing, of the intrigues and strategies employed by Cubans to resolve (as they say) their three daily problems: breakfast, lunch and dinner. Hunger does not dignify.

Can there really still be people in France dazzled by free education and healthcare in Cuba? Presumably there can be, otherwise the critic's recommendation would be redundant. And indeed my second (and so far last) visit to Cuba was with a group of French psychiatrists who had formed a Franco-Cuban psychiatric association. Admittedly this was now ten years ago, but I doubt whether any of them has changed his mind since.

They were many of them former companions of my wife at medical school in Paris during and after the effervescence of 1968. You could pick out the psychiatrists at the airport. 'There's one!' I would exclaim, pointing to a middle-aged man with a disorderly halo of white artificially curled hair, a little like that of those small white dogs that have become fashionable recently: and of course I was right. In fact, he was to give in Cuba one of the most memorable lectures I have ever heard. Its title was '*Can Psychoanalysis Survive?*', a pretty arcane question, to say the least, in a city (Havana) in which the buildings were collapsing and the power supply erratic, but it goes without saying that the lecture was incomprehensible by ordinary mortals. About twenty minutes into it, *le Frisé*, as my wife and I called him, suddenly stopped and said that he now realised that he had been reading out the pages of his lecture in the wrong order, though neither he nor anyone in the audience had noticed this until then. My wife and I, as well as an anaesthetist in the audience who was attending with his wife, a psychiatrist, were the only ones who laughed or found this in any way extraordinary: everyone else, apparently, found it perfectly normal. *Le Frisé* began again, no more comprehensibly than the first time; and when he had finished, the anaesthetist stood up, apologised for being but a literal-minded Cartesian, said, 'Your lecture is titled Can

Psychoanalysis Survive? Is the answer yes or no?'

Le Frisé was quite unembarrassed by this question.

'What have you heard?' he said.

The film, *Candelaria*, made by a Colombian, is not such as to please Castrophiles. It is, to quote again the review in *Le Monde des livres*, 'a Balzacian story, meticulous and engrossing, of the intrigues and stratagems' of Cuban daily life, which is not to say that it is strident in its political message. It assumes that everyone knows what it is talking about without having to explain the history or context.

The story is of an old couple, one of whom is a woman called Candelaria. She is white and her husband is black (incidentally, a subtle suggestion or hint that Castro was not responsible for an improvement in race relations, since this couple was married before he came to power). Although aged, she still works in the laundry of a hotel for tourists and at night in a bar where she sings, where her husband also works a little. At home, they are down to their last lightbulb and so take trouble to extend its life, mostly lighting their home by candle even when there is power. Occasionally we hear political speeches emanating from an old radio, intolerably dull and boring, all the more so after fifty years of such speeches. You can't eat national sovereignty or dignity; nor is personal dignity easy to maintain in conditions of perpetual surveillance by the Committees for the Defence of the Revolution, who pry into everyone's life.

Candelaria has some tiny chicks which she has surreptitiously raised in their dilapidated but surprisingly large flat in a crumbling building, but even this is against the law because they require feeding and will not only bring the state nothing, but — worse still — will bring private profit. The old couple have therefore to hide the chicks from the eyes of all those (who are many) who might denounce her as a profiteer and enemy of the revolution, an example of the intrusion of totalitarianism into the crevices of daily life. Such surveillance is both petty and thorough: the one being a necessary condition of the other.

The life of the old couple is otherwise peaceable, however, if hard and unsatisfying. They get by because he sells leaves of tobacco, taken from the cigar factory in which he works during the day, on the black market. But the tenor of their life is changed when she finds a video camera among the sheets which have been sent down in a bundle to the hotel's laundry. This is somewhat implausible, for it is unlikely that so bulky an item could go unnoticed until she, an ordinary laundrywoman, finds it. However, suspension of disbelief is often easy enough in the cinema.

After some twists and turns, the camera ends up in the warehouse of a large dealer in black market goods — large, that is, in Cuban terms. The dealer's warehouse is an Aladdin's cave of what anywhere else would be called old junk, but in Cuba is a repository of untold riches. It is presided over by a young and slimy type who anywhere else might be a hard salesman of real estate of dubious value to buyers who cannot afford it. But here in Havana he is a big wheel, never without his cigar, always with a supply of dollars, and with a manner suggesting that he knows what life is *really* about (swindle or be swindled). Having looked over the video camera — an object of incalculable value in Castro's Cuba — the dealer conceives of a new idea, typical of a certain kind of mental fertility.

Having gone through what was recorded while the camera was still in the old couple's possession, the dealer finds a sequence of Candelaria half-naked in bed. He has the sudden inspiration to make a geriatric pornographic film to sell and pays the couple what for Cuba is an astronomical sum in dollars. This allows them to buy such luxuries as chicken.

The idea being a great success, the dealer wants them to continue, but they decline to do so. They have their dignity — the real kind, not the ersatz kind shouted down the radio.

Alas, Candelaria then develops the symptoms of cancer. She needs money to pay for the chemotherapy that might or might not cure her or prolong her life (the doctor refuses to give a precise prognosis, in common with doctors everywhere). But so much for the free healthcare that the book-reviewer says still dazzles visitors to Cuba.

Candelaria, however, prefers to face her death directly, without any attempt to evade or postpone it, a choice that one feels she would have made even if she had not been obliged to prostitute herself to obtain the drugs that might have aided her.

The distinction between her personal dignity and the demagogic kind offered by Castro is clear. Hers is the result of choice made as an individual, his is the kind imposed by a dictator, though it would be against the evident truth of human feeling to deny that there can be such a thing as genuine national pride, both for good and for ill.

Resentment, however, of the type to which Castro appealed for half a century without ever letting up, is the most useless, indeed destructive, of emotions, though both durable and gratifying — in a sour way. When resentment is made ideology (with whatever justification or lack of it), as it has in Cuba and Venezuela, squalor — moral, economic, physical, psychological and spiritual — invariably and inevitably follows.

Candelaria and her husband rise above their conditions to achieve a true nobility. They do this by preserving a private sphere which it is the aim of all totalitarian regimes to destroy. We should not flatter ourselves, however, that we are immune from the totalitarian impulse or temptation, very much the contrary. Freedom gains no final or everlasting victory, especially where there is a large, frustrated intelligentsia.

13

L'ORDRE DES CHOSES, DIR. ANDREA SEGRE, ITALY AND LIBYA

All social policy harms someone; therefore, there is no perfect social policy, just as there is no perfect criminal justice system that convicts all the guilty and acquits all the innocent. It is inevitable, then, that all social policy can be criticised from the point of view of its victims and that, therefore, when disagreements over policy emerge as they always do, resort must be had both to abstract principle and to statistics to decide which policy on the whole is the worse.

The problem is even greater than this suggests, however, for the desiderata of social policy are incommensurable and even contradictory. On what scale does one weigh freedom against security or prosperity against stability? People may disagree not only about means but about ends; when opinions polarise, shrillness, bitterness and personal enmity increase.

In this film, a very senior officer of the Italian police and intelligence service, Corrado Rinaldi, is charged by a government minister with reducing the flow of migrants across the Mediterranean from the Libyan coast. This is a political necessity for the whole of Europe but particularly for Italy because popular discontent with seemingly uncontrolled immigration is growing. The plan is to establish large holding camps in Libya for those trying to cross the Mediterranean, administered by the Libyans and paid for by the Europeans. If a sufficiently high proportion of the migrants (or refugees) do not make it across, they will before long stop even trying to do so in the first place. The situation is complicated because the Libyans are deeply divided among themselves, the western allies having overthrown, or caused to be overthrown, the evil but in some ways effective dictator, Muammar Gaddafi. Rinaldi is soon caught in a personal, psychological and moral dilemma.

At first, we see him in Italy. My first thought, I have to admit, was that (if the film were accurate) the upper echelons of the Italian state live in considerable splendour, and it is scarcely any wonder that the country's public debt is so high. That debt is mainly held by Italians, who therefore assiduously save so that their ruling class may live in clover. Whether the senior civil servants really do live like the *haute bourgeoisie* I cannot say from personal knowledge.

Rinaldi is portrayed as a man of obsessive-compulsive disposition. We see him first wheeling his dustbin to be collected the next day from his elegant, immaculate and presumably very expensive house in a rich suburb. Then he crosses the road to adjust the dustbin of his neighbour so that it is disposed symmetrically against the garden wall. Several times in the film he adjusts things so that they are made symmetrical or in perfect alignment, from which we deduce that he is a man (unusually, perhaps, for an Italian) of a certain rigidity of mind, who desires an impossible perfection of the world.

He is sent to Tripoli to arrange matters with a local warlord who is an enemy of the Libyan government, such as it is. Libyan factions are divided by tribe and business interests: for them, people-trafficking and internment of captured migrants are virtually their only economic activity. To talk of human rights in this situation is like talking of the freedom of opinion of lions and gazelles.

With two other bureaucrats, one Italian and one French, Rinaldi visits a detention centre run by the Libyans. Somewhat implausibly, I thought, the guards mistreat the inmates in front of them. Perhaps by doing so they wish to show that they do not have the means to treat them better and that they need more money (from the European Union) to do so, or perhaps merely to display their diligence. Rinaldi, I must say, conducts himself like a pro-consul, with the arrogance of the representative of a superior or conquering power — an unfortunate manner, all the more so since Italy was once the colonising power in Libya. On the other hand, Libyan warlords are not the kind of people to respond to please and thank you: power and money are what they respect.

In war-torn Tripoli, Rinaldi finds himself a hotel the luxury of which I have never myself experienced. It is true that when a city is destroyed by bombardment or civil war the first thing to rise from the ashes or to be put back in order is the luxury hotel to welcome foreign dignitaries, senior aid workers and television journalists, and the first things to be imported are pink champagne and superior whisky, but all the same Rinaldi seems, for a public servant, to be lodged in very luxurious conditions indeed (and luxury in such places is doubly expensive).

While he walks through the women's section of the detention camp, a young Somali woman calls to him, gives him a computer memory card and asks him to deliver it to her uncle in Rome so that he will send money for her release. He complies with her request and delivers it to a café in Rome where Somalis gather. He is treated there with suspicion, of course, suspected of being an official who is intent on discovering illegal immigrants to be deported. Nevertheless, the memory card is passed on to the uncle.

Not surprisingly, Rinaldi has downloaded and looked at the contents of the memory card. He hears the young woman's recorded prayer asking for God's assistance and protection in making the hazardous journey to Europe. He writes an e-mail to her and a little later she calls him on Skype. She tells him that her husband and brother are in Finland — her husband is a university student of mathematics — and that she would like to join them. She asks for his aid in doing so. She also asks him to show her Rome from his window: he holds up the computer screen to show her the beautiful view from his window.

He returns to Libya in a further attempt to get the Libyans to co-operate in controlling the flow of migrants. While there, he sees his Somali interlocutor again, this time being herded from one place to another like an animal. She sees him and beseeches his help, which he promises her. But it quickly emerges that the only way in which he can help her is by bribing the Libyan warlord who controls the migrant camp. After soul-searching, he decides not to do so. The last scene in the film is of him dining at home in his large and elegant house with his wife and two children. The contrast between his life and that of the internment camp could hardly be greater.

We do not know the reason for his failure to help her: whether it is because, if he had done so, he would have been open to blackmail by the warlord, or whether he decided it was wrong in principle. But I, at any rate, felt that the contrast between his clean and luxurious life on the one hand, and the life of the migrant, was something of an emotional manipulation, in so far as if he had extracted the woman and brought her to Europe, it was not such as he who would have suffered the consequences but rather the people among whom she would have settled: come what might, he would have continued to lead his clean and luxurious existence. It is all too easy to be on the side of the angels when the bill is paid by someone else.

There are slight implausibilities about the film to which I find it difficult to affix the correct significance. For example, Rinaldi is never seen in Libya dressed other than elegantly, usually in his well-cut business suit. Indeed, he walks on the beach in such a suit, but the heat affects neither his comfort nor his smartness. He seems to carry air-conditioning around with him. Not a bead of sweat emerges from his brow in the burning heat, and he makes no gesture of discomfort. Moreover, he gives the impression of representing a country in which political intrigue, skulduggery and corruption are unknown, in which everything is done strictly according to law. This impression is given in order to maintain the vast social and economic distance between the lives of the migrants and those of Europeans, a distance which the latter are determined selfishly to protect.

Still, the film does raise acutely the current problems of mass migration to Europe from Africa and the Middle East. I saw the dilemmas in my work as a doctor: for while I sympathised with the migrants as individuals, I did not much care for the transformations their further mass influx would bring about.

Sometimes in my work I would be consulted by illegal immigrants who would ask me to care for members of their families. This I was supposed, officially, not to do, but I did it anyway, because as a doctor I saw only the individuals before me. In many cases, also, they struck me as in some ways better than the local population. Moreover, the idea that they were by nature and vocation spongers, come to take advantage of the Welfare State, was mostly untrue: they wanted to work, and those who did so, though it was illegal, seemed better adjusted than those asylum-seekers who merely complied with the regulations laid down for them on their arrival. I am not economist enough to know whether the labour of illegal migrants, being mostly unskilled, depressed wages in general, but it seemed to me that those who argued that such immigrants were economically beneficial because they added to the growth of the GDP mistook the point. It is the GDP *per head* that counts, to say nothing of the other effects of large influxes of migrants.

Whenever I meet a Somali taxi-driver in England, I am pleased to reminisce with him about my sole visit to Somalia. Perhaps I delude myself, but it seems to give him pleasure too, for it is surely not very often that he meets a person who could find Somalia on a map, let alone has been there. Life for a Somali taxi-driver in England cannot be easy, and so a conversation about his home country with someone who knows even a little of it must come as something of a relief from loneliness and the feeling of being perpetually an alien.

For all this, however, I would not want the small market town in which I live to be transformed by the arrival of, say, a thousand Somalis. I am content with my town as it is, which is why I chose it as a place to live. No doubt this might seem reprehensible to those who want to be pure citizens of the world rather than of anywhere in particular, but contentment with certain arrangements as they are is as much a social virtue as it is a manifestation of complacent bigotry. The desire for profound change is not a virtue in itself; and while I welcome strangers, I do not want to be a stranger in my own country.

My short visit to Somalia, incidentally, taught me a lesson or two, for example that those who claim to work for humanity do not always do so, nor are they devoid of personal interest just because they are humanitarians.

It was in Siad Barre's time. He was a terrible dictator, of course, but terrible dictatorships have a tendency in that part of the world to become, retrospectively, a golden age by comparison with what comes after. There was a cholera epidemic raging outside Mogadishu, the capital, and I went to the offices of the United Nations High Commission for Refugees (the UNHCR) to inform myself about it, but there was no one there to talk to, because the staff were on strike.

According to a notice, they had two grievances: the first was that the portions of food in the canteen were too small, and the second, more important, was that the Somali government was trying to force them to exchange their salaries, paid if I remember rightly in Swiss francs, at the official rather than the black (or open) market rate for Somali shillings. There was a dialectic at work: the humanitarians wanted to live luxuriously as cheaply as possible, while the Somalis, or the Somali government, wanted to exploit them as a source of foreign funds. A mere cholera epidemic was a matter of small consequence to either of these parties. Thus, the recent scandals at Oxfam did not surprise me in the least.

If the director of *L'Ordre des choses* intended the viewer to harbour only feelings of sympathy for the young Somali woman in the internment camp, he was not successful, at least not with me. Her manner lacked charm but more than that, Somalia is a long way from Libya and she, or someone else in her family, must have paid a lot for her to get there. Where did the money come from? She also had a sophisticated computer, knew how to use it, had a memory card and a Skype account, spoke excellent English, and was therefore a member of a privileged class in Somalia. There is a strong possibility that such a privileged person belonged to a ruthless (if losing) clan and was far from the poorest of the poor, one of the wretched of the earth, though it is also possible that she was trying to escape some personal trauma. But still, one would have liked more information about her personal history before according her blanket sympathy; and the film not only failed to provide it but failed to notice that it ought to be provided.

We knew, of course, that it would be better for her to get to Finland, but would it be better for Finland? That is a far more difficult question, so difficult that we avert our minds from it. We also avert our minds from the possibility that an increase in prosperity in Africa (often touted as the solution to the problem) will result not in fewer but in more African migrants to Europe — insofar as more of them would be able to pay for the passage, like the young Somali woman in this film.

14

FROST, DIR. SHARUNAS BARTAS, LITHUANIA

My only visit to Lithuania was on the eve of its liberation from the Soviet Union. It was an exhilarating moment. The *Sajudis* movement, led by Professor Landsbergis, the musician and musicologist who was to become the country's first post-Soviet president (and whom I met briefly before that), was at its apogee. It could have been defeated only by force, which the leaders of the Soviet Union no longer had the confidence or ruthlessness to use. It is very rarely that one experiences an unmistakable and quick transformation for the better in a country: and, indeed, I have never experienced it anywhere else, except in Latvia and Estonia, where it was happening at the same time.

Of course, Lithuania had its own dark history. I felt slightly uneasy when audiences applauded old newsreels of Antanas Smetona, the interwar dictator of the country[6], and even worse when I heard antisemitic remarks, despite the fact that the Jews of Lithuania had been almost entirely exterminated

---

[6] By far not the worst of dictators, however.

during the Second World War with the considerable, not to say the enthusiastic, assistance of the local population. Still, that was more than four decades earlier, and the members and supporters of *Sajudis* were not responsible for what was done in those years, and the Landsbergis family was a notably honourable one. There was no disputing the fact, moreover, that the populations of the Baltic states suffered terribly under Soviet rule, experiencing two bouts of mass deportation in a few years. A professor there told me that when he came out of school in Vilnius there would a flatbed truck waiting outside, and if a child's parents were on it the child would have to climb aboard and would never be heard of again. Even at an early age, you knew not to ask questions about these disappearances.

In view of their recent history and current developments, it is not surprising that the Baltic states, though members of the European Union, are a little nervous. If Russia were to invade, membership of the Union would be about as much protection as a tissue handkerchief in a thunderstorm. The independence of the Baltic states is by grace and favour, and the presence of a large population of Russians in each of them could easily be used at any time to manufacture a *casus belli* (on a more recent visit to Riga, capital of Latvia, the majority of whose population in Russian, I saw not a word of Russian on any poster or building).

Frost is a film that takes the looming Russian threat as a kind of meteorological given. It is as if it were inherent in the Russian state to expand territorially whenever and wherever possible, and to retreat only when circumstances force it to do so. It is in a slightly expansionary phase at the moment:

Crimea, Georgia, the Ukraine. Of course, from the Russian point of view it is only reacting to encirclement; being without natural borders, it thinks its neighbours wish to dismember it.

In the film, a young couple called Rokas and Inga are asked by a friend to take a vanload of humanitarian aid — shoes and clothes — from Lithuania to the Ukraine, where it is to be delivered to the Ukrainian army. The journey is a long and difficult one, undertaken at the beginning of winter. The couple live together but hardly seem to be in love: they discover their love for one another at the end of the journey when it will be too late. *En route*, in fact, the girl betrays the boy by having a one-night stand with a contact in the Ukraine.

The plot is somewhat implausible. Taking shoes and clothes to an army, even if it is fighting what you consider a good fight, can hardly count as humanitarian aid. Moreover, the Ukrainian army, underequipped as it might be, can hardly stand in need of civilian shoes and clothes. It has tanks and armoured vehicles and communication equipment and artillery. Its soldiers are dressed in proper camouflage, with helmets and body-armour. It is fighting a war with Russian separatists who want at least autonomy, and more likely annexation by Russia, for those areas in the east where the Russians are in the majority. They want to make Ukraine as currently constituted untenable. The war is vicious (few wars are not), fought in the most depressing conditions, the hundreds of thousands of square miles of mess left by the Soviet Union.

The couple drive through some of the most dispiriting landscapes in the world. It is not only that the land is flat and featureless, but that it has been subjected to the shoddiest of all human civilizations. No one who has not driven through some part of the former Soviet Union can have any idea of its depressing ugliness. Nothing has been done properly, with care or affection, let alone with pride: not the fencing, not the ploughing, not the road-building, not the construction, not even the erection of telegraph poles. It is a landscape of slush and mud, the buildings dilapidated even before they are completed (which they rarely are). Aesthetics have long counted for nothing in this universe of irredeemable shoddiness, which the destruction wrought by war only serves to emphasise and bring to completion.

Not yet at the front, Rokas and Inga stop off at a small Ukrainian army camp presided over by a colonel with whom they have a philosophical discussion. Would Rokas be prepared to fight to defend Lithuania from the Russians? He is not sure. The colonel points out the contradiction: Rokas is prepared to take a dangerous journey to supply Ukraine but is uncertain whether he would fight to preserve Lithuanian independence. Perhaps the difference is in the chances of success in the struggle.

The Ukraine is a large country with a large population and at least some remnant of a powerful army. Lithuania is tiny both geographically and in population. Resistance, however heroic, would be futile (watching the dictator, Smetona, inspecting his toy army during the inter-war years would be enough to persuade you of that). Calling on people to die for a lost cause is usually a lost cause.

The colonel with whom Rokas has his discussion has a Russian father and Ukrainian mother and says that he is defending what is 'ours'. He says that he hates war nevertheless, and describes its horrors, among which is the recovery of bodies killed in action. In summer, he says, the smell is indescribable. As he spoke, oddly enough, I was taken back to my childhood, when my father had an accounts clerk, Mr. B....., who always dressed in a dark suit and black shoes so highly polished that they were like looking glasses. He always had a bowler hat and a furled umbrella, a bit like Major Thompson. His ability to add up a long list of figures by running a pencil over them without touching the paper impressed me (this was still the days of pounds, shillings and pence). He added faster than any adding machine of the time and never made a mistake. It was a *tour de force*, of a limited kind.

He was the soul of respectability, but one lunchtime, when I walked with him in the park, he told me that he had been an accountant of a kind in the army: it had been his job to count the bodies after a battle, such as that at El Alamein. He said he had never been so busy.

He had also shot someone dead, which as a boy I found very impressive. He was not proud of it however, rather the reverse. It was a German soldier, and he had been unsure whether or not he was in the process of surrendering to, or attacking, him. He decided to take no chances and shot him dead. His action had troubled him ever since. Had he been right? Had he been wrong? There was no way now of ever knowing.

My brief acquaintance with Mr B..... taught me that the dullest exterior may conceal a tormented interior. I wish I could find him — he would now be in his later nineties, if still alive — to tell him how much our acquaintance had meant to me.

The young Lithuanian couple reach the front where the situation is so tense that they are, understandably, received with suspicion rather than with joy or gratitude, though they nevertheless manage to deliver their goods.

One of the merits of the film is that the violence in which it ends is not in the least glamourized or even slightly sanitised. It is realistic to the point that one can almost smell the blood, a smell that no doctor could mistake.

The morning after their mission has been accomplished, Rokas wakes early and asks one of the Ukrainian soldiers to show him the demarcation line, a few hundred yards from where he has spent the night, that currently separates the two sides in the war. Rokas wants to take photos of it on his phone, presumably to boast of his adventure to his friends and family back home. In order to see the demarcation line, he and the soldier have to climb on to the flat roof of a disused factory, disused as so many factories now are in the former communist countries of Europe.

There was nothing more expressive of communist incompetence and waste than the abandonment of factories that produced nothing that anyone wanted the moment an alternative was available. Some time after the downfall of Ceausescu in Romania, I saw a wonderful exhibition of photographs of disused factories in that country, fallen almost immediately into ruins of an unromantic kind. They were built and located not according to any economic reason, but for propagandistic or ideological reasons: for communists, as I remember from friendships with communists and from the study of communist iconography, a tall chimney belching polluting smoke in the midst of the countryside represented progress. Indeed, some factories in communist times seemed to produce little else but pollution.

As in the film, the factories in Romania were reduce to concrete and twisted steel skeletons of enormous size, standing as often as not in pools of oily mud of different phosphorescent shades. But in the film when Rokas and the Ukrainian soldier climb on to the roof, a Russian shot rings out. They scramble to escape, but after a few more shots and an explosion in the factory, the soldier is killed. Rokas too is hit, but at first is able to continue making his escape back to the Ukrainian lines. As he tries to reach them, however, another shot rings out and he is hit in the thigh. This is so well-done that one almost feels hit in the thigh oneself, as Adam Smith's *The Theory of Moral Sentiments* leads us to suppose that it would. Rokas falls to the ground in the snow, and losing blood quickly becomes slightly delirious, hallucinating Inga and speaking to her as if she were present. Then he dies. It is a fine, affecting and realistic piece of acting, and recalls Mistress Quickly's account of Falstaff's death — so vivid that we come to believe that Falstaff actually makes an appearance in *Henry V.*

The young man has died for nothing. He is not even a journalist who might have thought the story worth the risk of death. But young men are like that (I was myself): if they see a risk, they take it almost because it is there, and do not really believe in the possibility of their own death. Many of us besides think that we do not know who we truly are until we have faced danger, our lives until then being all veneer.

I don't suppose many Lithuanians require much warning about the danger next door, but the film may at least encourage them to declare their love before it is too late.

15

JERSEY AFFAIRE, Dir. Michael Pearce, Jersey

I had intended, when I started this book, to include no films
from my own country, but I decided, with resort to mental
legalism, that I could allow a film located in the island of
Jersey. Though Jersey has been a possession of the English
crown for nearly a thousand years, it is, strictly speaking, not
part of the United Kingdom. When the islanders go to
England, they speak of going to the U.K. Moreover, there is a
customs border between the Channel Islands and Britain.
They have never been members of the European Union,
either.

Such was my excuse for breaking my self-imposed rule, but
I also had special reasons for wanting to include this film. In
the *Officiel des spectacles*, the weekly listing of films, plays,
exhibitions and other events in Paris, *Jersey Affaire* was
described as follows:

> While a serial killer strikes in Jersey, a young woman
> defies her parents by going out with a young man of modest
> background with a criminal record.

The English title of the film is *Beast*, and in the section of my library devoted to crime there is a book titled *The Beast of Jersey* by Joan Paisnel, the wife of the Beast, a man who for ten years between 1960 and 1971 (as yesterday to me) terrorised the island by entering houses in a rubber mask and sexually assaulting women and children. The terror caused on so small an island, where almost everyone is known to almost everyone else, may easily be imagined.

I also lived for several months on Jersey while my wife worked as a replacement doctor there. To pass the time I researched and wrote a book about three murders on Jersey that took place in quick succession in the 1840s, the first of them the stabbing to death of George Le Cronier, the only policemen to have been killed in Jersey, by Madame Le Gendre, a brothel-keeper of Mulberry Cottage (which still stands under that name). Another of the murders was by a mad hatter, probably sent mad by the mercury with which he smoothed the felt of his hats. All three murderers were transported to Van Diemen's Land, where at least two of them flourished. I discovered from my researches that the Victorians, at least on the island of Jersey, were a good deal less anxious to impose the death penalty than I had supposed, indeed quite the opposite. Madame Le Gendre in particular had no extenuating circumstances and there was no strictly legal reason why she should have escaped the gallows, for her crime was as premeditated as it was possible for a crime to be. But executions in those days were in public and the authorities thought that the spectacle of hanging a woman was especially unedifying to the public. She departed Jersey finely dressed, while agitating her handkerchief from the deck of the ship to a baying crowd of ill-wishers on the quayside.

My wife and I had been extremely happy on Jersey (I returned to give a talk to the *Société Jersiaise*), and even a merely cinematic return would be a pleasure to us, albeit for a film about serious crime.

In addition, the subject interested me. I had noticed while a prison doctor that particularly vicious murderers, if publicity had been given to their crimes, were seldom without declarations of love or offers of marriage, usually by post, from women who did not know them and had never met them. Sometimes prison visitors, who undertook their visiting from a variety of motives, some of them no doubt hidden from themselves, fell in love with prisoners and married them. Needless to say, they never fell in love with recidivist petty criminals, shoplifters or the like: it was the big fish they hoped to catch and no doubt save. The greater the sinner, the greater the saint, that was their belief. They believed that 'he will change for me' — a kind of grandiosity that some psychiatrists share. In Australia, I met a journalist called Jacqelynne Wilcox-Bailey who had interviewed women prison visitors who had married the murderers they visited. Their stories were of self-deception of a scarcely credible degree. A pair of middle-class sisters, for example, bored with their comfortable bourgeois existence, went prison visiting and each of them married a wife-murderer. The first was murdered by her new husband three days after his release, everything having gone well till then; the second was then very nearly killed by *her* new husband shortly after *his* release, rescued just in time by her neighbours. Her comment on her experience was, 'I think our relationship has been strengthened by all that we have gone through', or words to that effect.

The tedium of bourgeois existence, especially in a society as inevitably constricting as Jersey's, is what attracts the protagonist Moll to Pascal Renouf, a man of a very different type from those among whom she normally moves. He is a rugged outdoor type who knows how to chop logs and shoot hares. (Are there hares in Jersey? I never saw any, or anywhere they were likely to be found[7].)

One of the disappointments of the film for my wife and I was that, apart from the coastal scenes, little of it appeared to have been filmed on the island, and we were therefore cheated of our nostalgia.

The manners of Moll's new friend, Pascal, are rough, and he antagonises Moll's ferociously bourgeois mother. He is supposed to be authentic while she is but a flimsy construction of her social role. It goes without saying that we are supposed to sympathise with his uncouthness rather than with her hypocritical and insincere social polish.

Moll has always been something of a rebel; indeed, rebellion resides in her hair, which is red. (Her mother's is blond: no cliché is left unturned.) At school, from which she was expelled, she stabbed a girl with a pair of scissors, after

---

[7] I thought the depiction in the film of wide-open spaces both a geographical and an artistic mistake. Jersey is small, about 45 square miles, with a population of 90,000. At 2,000 inhabitants per square mile, there are no wide-open spaces. Moreover, the depiction of such spaces lessens the claustrophobic atmosphere of menace that would have been achieved by a more realistic depiction of the island.

which her mother gave up work to school her at home. Moll is clever but wayward — or is it wayward because clever, or clever because wayward? In one of the least convincing scenes in the film, she goes later in life to the store now owned by the girl she once stabbed to apologise to her, allegedly meeting her for the first time since having done so. This would be quite impossible in Jersey: after less than a month there, I began to greet people in the street whom I already knew. It is both the comfort and curse of small places that you are never quite anonymous.

A Jersey policeman, who happens to be in unrequited love with Moll, informs her that Pascal has a criminal record, including for a sexual assault on a fourteen-year-old girl, for which he has served time in prison. Again, it is unlikely that she would not already have known this: everyone knows everything in Jersey, including things that are not true.

The action takes place while a serial killer is on the loose. He kills a fourth victim, whose corpse is found in a potato field, her mother stuffed with earth. Pascal Renouf is strongly suspected of the crime and before long is arrested. Moll lies to the police about his whereabouts at the material time, and he is released, a Portuguese farm labourer being arrested in his place. (Ten per cent of Jersey's population comes from Madeira, a migration which had not failed to result in tensions and prejudice.)

Happily reunited, Moll and Renouf go to a nightclub where she informs him that she would like to leave the island which she finds so stifling. This, at least, is highly credible. Nevertheless, they quarrel: he has his life on the island, a small business as a handyman. Angered by her causal announcement that she wants to leave and for him to accompany her, he very nearly strangles her. They separate for a few days, but even though she now realises that he is in fact the serial killer terrorising Jersey, she goes back to him.

This, too, is credible. How many times in my career did I encounter something similar? In particular, I remember a woman who had had her jaw broken by her lover, a man who had recently come out of prison after having served a sentence for the murder of a previous lover. Fracturing her jaw was not the first time he had injured her; he had also broken her arm. But despite all our warnings and efforts to help her, she returned to him, and the last I saw of her was with him walking hand-in-hand down the hospital corridor. Love is a many-dangered thing.

As with my patient and her violent lover, we see Moll and Pascal walk hand-in-hand. She has by now confessed to him her knowledge that he is the serial killer, but she believes that he has changed; she knows people can change because she was once like him. When she stabbed the girl at school, she did not do so, as she previously claimed, in an access of rage because she was being bullied, but because she wanted to kill. 'We are two of a type,' she says.

This supposed equivalence, it seems to me, weakens the film rather than strengthens it, for it undermines the uncomfortable message that some women are not only attracted to evil men, but to men whom they know to be evil, and that therefore they are complicit in their own victimisation. This does not excuse the evil men, of course, but it is something that is unmentionable in polite society because it falls under the rubric of blaming the victim. That an intelligent, middle-class girl could be attracted to a serial killer *because* he is a serial killer and not because she is herself a potential serial killer is a far more unsettling thought than the film's storyline suggests.

The anti-bourgeois stance of the film irritated me somewhat. (You can never go far wrong with a bourgeois audience in attacking the bourgeoisie.) It relied on cliché and caricature to do so, such as the tinkling of crystal glasses and china cups, and pointless boring conversations in which nothing is either said or meant. But is non-bourgeois conversation so very much better? Pascal Renouf hardly says anything interesting either. He smoulders sexually, as in a romantic novel, but how long can such smouldering last? I have not myself observed that conversation in proletarian pubs is much more interesting than that around bourgeois tea-tables or the vapidities expressed at garden parties. The fact is that a great deal of what people say is either redundant or boring, vapid or empty. That is why malice is so often necessary and comes as a relief.

16

SUGARLAND, DIR. DAMON GAMEAU, AUSTRALIA

Australians, so it is said, are the second fattest people in the world, after the Americans, while the British are the fattest in Europe. The reasons for this are worth pondering, all the more so since the rest of the world has the unfortunate tendency to follow blindly where the English-speakers lead. English is the *lingua franca* of the world, and Anglo-Saxon bad habits and bad taste become the bad habits and bad taste of the world.

In matters of food, that taste is not only bad, but crude and childish. This film, whose object is to alert us to the dangers of sugar, now omnipresent in our diet, begins by exhibiting Australian confectionary. Not only is it vast in quantity, but coloured by nothing found in nature, if by nature we mean products that are not too many stages removed from animal, vegetable or unrefined mineral. Australian confectionary, at least as depicted here, is sky-blue, baby-pink and other such bright and garish colours, as if people were guided by their eyes in what they ate, moreover by eyes without the capacity for subtler aesthetic judgment, childish or magpie eyes that respond to the immediate attraction of brightness. How is it that so many people, especially in the Anglo-Saxon world, have never become aesthetically adult, and remain so unsophisticated in their tastes?

Part of the answer, perhaps, is in the prevalence of plastic. Plastic toys and even plastic public playgrounds, crudely coloured, fashioned in moulds without care or attention, no doubt attract children as flowers attract pollinating insects (which have better taste, however). I have noticed that the iconography of Winnie-the-Pooh is now completely dominated by Disney's crude and brightly coloured renderings while the subtle and tender Ernest Shepherd illustrations have fallen into desuetude. No doubt parents might reply that children prefer the former to the latter, without realising that this would be precisely an argument for, not against, the latter. Parents are supposed not merely to entertain but to educate, and not always to take the line of least resistance. Aesthetic education is of importance.

It is also in the choice of food that one sees the transfer of authority from the parent to the child. Often one sees children as young as three being asked by their mothers what they would like to eat. Evolutionists never tire of telling us that we are predisposed by evolution itself to like sweet and fatty foods because we grew up (as a species) in the savannahs of Africa, where food was scarce, and by psychologists that sugar and fat provide the most immediate gratification when we are hungry. Whether or not this is a correct explanation, the fact is that most children will, if given the chance, choose food that is not nutritionally the best for them. Freedom of choice is an excellent thing, but it should be an educated choice. And if that choice is never educated, it is small wonder that adults may be attracted to fatty, sweet doughnuts with icing the colours of the rainbow (only brighter). I remember my mother saying to me, after trying a bad ice-cream against her better judgment, 'This ice-cream tastes pink.'

Sugarland is irritatingly demotic in its presentation but is serious nonetheless. Its narrator decides to follow a diet that contains as much sugar as the average Australian consumes, that is to say forty teaspoonsful daily, without resort to the most obviously unhealthy and sugar-laden products. Prior to this, he had avoided sugar; he wanted to find out experimentally what sixty days of sugar would do to him.

The film's premise, that we live in an increasingly sugared world, is surely correct. I have noticed it in small ways. Dishes in Indian restaurants now often have added sugar, and indeed their menus advertise a sweet taste as an attraction to certain diners. Even dishes not advertised as sweet in taste often have sugar added; sweet dishes must be sweet indeed. Bread in America often tastes to me more like cake than bread; at an expensive hotel, attending a conference for upper-middle class intellectuals, I could find nothing at breakfast that was not sweet, and when I asked for something that was not sweet was told that nothing was available, my request itself being regarded as very odd. When American authors seek an image of irresistibility, they almost always resort to chocolate cake, as if no one could resist it in any circumstances whatever. And, because I like grapefruit, I have noticed that it is increasingly difficult to find the white variety, having been replaced on the market by the sweeter pink. Indeed, in France (which generally lags the Anglo-Saxon world in the consumption of sugar, as it once lagged in the prevalence of tattoos), I noticed recently some bright green grapefruit with the brand name of *Sweetie*, when the whole point of grapefruit is — for me, at least — that they are sour rather than sweet.

So sugar is gaining entry everywhere and is causatively related to the epidemic of obesity and late-onset diabetes (relatively late, that is, though decreasingly so), that threatens, for the first time in a century, give or take a world war or two, to reverse the continuous rise in life expectancy in the developed world.

It is a pity, and perhaps an injustice, that the film has only a short historical clip of Professor John Yudkin, the British biochemist, who warned against the dangers of sugar long ago and in 1972 published a book about refined sugar called *Pure, White and Deadly*. I remember its first edition being remaindered in a bookshop in the Charing Cross Road, though a copy is now unobtainable and would cost a great deal; and though the theory was more or less pooh-poohed at the time, the book has become a classic since. Yudkin was derided at the time by Ancel Keys, the American physiologist, who favoured fat rather than sugar as the source of all evil and claimed that Yudkin, apart from his epidemiological data that applied to whole populations but not to individual patients, had no theory as to why sugar should be so bad for health. At least in the short-term, Keys won the argument, in the sense that he had more direct influence on both public opinion and policy, but more than twenty years after Yudkin's death, it is he who appears the far greater figure.

The protagonist of the film found that, while the number of

calories that he consumed remained constant[8], he put on weight very quickly (and visibly) when he included the average intake of sugar in his diet. Moreover, certain of his blood indices, particularly of his liver function, deteriorated markedly and very rapidly. He soon showed signs of fatty liver, a precursor of illnesses both hepatic and non-hepatic. The good news was that these changes were rapidly reversed once he returned to a non-sugary diet.

He noted psychological changes in himself as well while he ate sugar. He became more lethargic in general and given to swings of mood. These he attributed to sugar because they seemed to follow the pattern of his consumption: high mood when he had just consumed sugar and low when he was due for his next dose. Here the evidence was much less satisfactory because, of course, he was not blinded to his own sugar intake: he knew exactly when he had taken some. If he started out, as seems to me very likely that he did, with the idea that sugar affects mood, his so-called mood-swings (an expression I detest for reasons that I cannot go into here) were a self-fulfilling prophecy.

In the course of the film, the protagonist goes to the world capital of sugar, as of so many other things both good and bad, the United States, and finds that his problem there is not so much finding enough sweetened but otherwise not obviously unhealthy foods to reach his target of forty teaspoonsful of sugar daily, as of not grossly exceeding his target amount even when eating 'normally'. Avoiding sugar in much of America

---

[8] He also maintained his customary level of exercise.

is like avoiding bullets on a battlefield: without enormous effort it is almost impossible, and success is not certain even then.

The film omits quite a lot, as I suppose every documentary must, but omissions are just as eloquent as inclusions. The protagonist goes to the Appalachians, well-known for the degradation (as most people see it) of the population. Here he finds people who drink enormous quantities of sweetened drinks, one in particular called *Mountain Dew*, a bottle of which contains, if I remember correctly, more than a hundred and twenty teaspoonsful of sugar. Appalachian mothers give this stuff to their very young children, with not very surprising consequences. We hear a local dentist, who has fitted up a mobile clinic in which he drives to the small towns of the area, removing the rotted stumps of teeth in an eighteen-year-old's mouth. At that age, he will be fitted with false teeth.

One of the messages of the film is that the processed-food companies have conspired to make us dependent on or addicted to sugar, and then to deny that sugar is harmful, or at least more harmful than anything else. The companies have researched, for example, the sugar content (very high) that would most please us, and then put it in their products. And, claimed the film, sugar is addictive. It is the morally criminal but commercially successful induction of addiction to sugar that is responsible for the epidemic of obesity: obesity that would once have been considered grotesque but has now become almost normal.[9]

The film also contains an attack on the notion of personal responsibility, as if the manipulations of large corporations exonerated us and relieved us of any responsibility for our own condition. In other words, either we or corporations are responsible for ourselves, and since the corporations are, we are not. It is all their fault.

I have little doubt of corporations' potential for villainy (after all, they are run by humans), of their willingness to disregard the common good for their own sectional interest. At the same time, to regard obesity as having nothing to do with personal responsibility or choice seems to me, well, irresponsibly condescending to the great mass of the people. It suggests that no one can do anything for himself such as abandoning sugar-laden drinks. Eating pink- or blue-iced doughnuts is a fatality, not a choice, and the only way to stop people from eating them is to forbid their production in the first place.

At the same time, nutritional education is proposed as part of the solution, which implies that, after all, consumption of sugar has something to do with volition, even where the choice is bad or ill-informed. However, if the experience of tobacco control is anything to go by, the effect of education will be

---

[9] Honoré Daumier has a moving caricature, obviously based upon observed reality, of a very fat woman exhibited as a circus freak, and Daumier, a man of deep humanity, shows very clearly the sorrow of being exhibited as a freak. But in American cities, and now British and Australian, it is common to see people considerably fatter than Daumier's model, indeed they are numerous.

greatest on those who least need it, namely the better-educated who are already least inclined to overdose on sugar and whose tastes are relatively sophisticated. In so far as nutritional education would have any effect, therefore, it would serve to widen the gap between the richest and poorest deciles of the population, and such a widening would then be taken as evidence of social injustice.

Be that as it may, the premise of health education is that people are able to alter their behaviour in the light of the information they receive. As to legislation forcing the food companies to reduce the sugar content of their disgusting products (that is to say, products that disgust *me*), I have no objection. If anyone were to object that this would lower the GDP, assuming that the calculation could be made, I should reply that GDP is not the highest goal or good of humanity. Perhaps child pornography would increase the GDP, but we should not therefore permit it.

Sugarland, in its rather irritating way, does raise important questions of group or corporate responsibility on the one hand, and personal responsibility on the other. If ordinary people, especially if they are poor, can only be victims and not responsible agents, needing intellectuals and bureaucrats to save them, what price democracy?

Before I leave *Sugarland*, I must mention that throughout it I was awaiting the appearance of an eminent Australian professor whom I met briefly on a couple of occasions nearly forty years ago, Professor Paul Zimmet. He it was who conducted research on the island of Nauru in the Central Pacific (where I met him). The Nauruans had suddenly become very rich when they gained control of the phosphate deposits on the island (until then controlled by the British Phosphate Commission, comprising British, Australian and New Zealand interests). From being a people who subsisted on fish and coconuts, they went straight to being rich rentiers; and having nothing much else to do, they ate and drank. Having a sweet tooth, they drank vast quantities of Fanta and Château Yquem. They also ate vast piles of rice. Fifty per cent of the population contracted type II diabetes and though for a time the richest people in the world *per capita*, their life expectancy was less than 50. With great prescience, Professor Zimmet investigated the phenomena, as if he knew that he was seeing the future of his own country among others.

I remember thinking at the time that his research was an exercise in academic irrelevance and an excuse for a pleasant jaunt. I was pleased when, so much later, I saw him in this film, an honoured man. How wrong I had been!

17

THE BATTLESHIP ISLAND, DIR. RYOO SEUNG-WAN, KOREA

I have been to Korea only once, and that was to the North rather than the South. It was so terrible that, though Russia had yet to emerge from the dark night of communism, when I arrived back in Moscow from Pyongyang, I felt that I breathed free again — relatively-speaking, that is.

One very soon both grasps and tires of the official history of North Korea, repeated *ad nauseam* and on every possible occasion and some impossible ones, too. The then leader, Kim Il-Sung, the first of his dynasty (and still President, twenty-four years after his death), was deified as a great guerrilla leader, almost solely responsible for the defeat of the Japanese on the Korean peninsula, being the national saviour and liberator. But he was no more a liberator than he had been a guerrilla, having spent most of the war in the Soviet Union, which was not even at war with Japan; and the very idea that the man at the head of the most inhuman and tyrannical regime in the world should pose as a *liberator*, of all things, was enough to make the gorge rise.

But if there is one thing on which the two Koreas can

agree[10], it is on the brutality of the Japanese occupation which lasted thirty-five years. No doubt historical memory is always exploited, or at least is always exploitable, for contemporary political purposes, and is so exploited more crudely in the North than in the South, but this can hardly alter the fact that the Japanese occupation *was* of great brutality, albeit that it brought with it considerable economic development. Better to be left to one's own backwardness than driven into modernity at the end of a whip.[11]

This South Korean war film is nothing if not on a grand or epic scale. It is set on a small island, Hashima (the Battleship Island of the title), ten miles out to sea from Nagasaki. It was called Battleship Island because, at a distance, it has the appearance or profile of a late Nineteenth Century battleship. Coal was discovered there below sea level, and a mine worked from 1880 until 1974, when it was closed by its owners, Mitsubishi. For a time, it was the most crowded place on earth; more recently its ruined concrete buildings and other installations (mines with shafts three fifths of a mile deep) have been declared a World Heritage Site and turned into a tourist attraction. Certainly, Battleship Island is testimony to the breakneck speed and determination, as well as the human cost, of Japanese industrialisation.

----

[10] Just as the one thing upon which the Chinese and Japanese agree is a low opinion of the Koreans.

[11] The supposed backwardness of Japan before the arrival of Commodore Perry seems to me to indicate a very one-dimensional idea of backwardness. Before Perry's arrival, Japan had a very sophisticated culture, in many ways more refined than Perry's.

For the sake of this film, the makers constructed a replica of the island two thirds its size. When I learned of this, I was reminded of the time I arrived at Lambaréné in Gabon to discover that German film-makers there had constructed a replica of Dr Schweitzer's mission hospital right next to the original itself, though a good deal more salubrious than the original. None of the viewers of the film about Dr Schweitzer would have known this, of course, nor would it have affected their suspension of disbelief if they had known it. The actor who played Dr Schweitzer, I must say, looked the part to perfection with his crumpled tropical linen suit and drooping white moustache, a face once as familiar in the West as that of Einstein, a kind of ideogram or hieroglyph of humanitarian self-sacrifice, though I think very few people under the age of fifty could now identify him and the philosophical basis of his action has now been overthrown completely. By contrast, the Japanese occupation of Korea has never disappeared from Korean national consciousness, so traumatic was it.

During the Second World War, the mines of Battleship Island were worked by conscript, almost slave, labour, much of it Korean. It is said that fifteen hundred Koreans lost their lives there through accident, illness, malnutrition and maltreatment. It was because the information originally made available to tourists to the island failed to mention this episode in the island's history that the South Korean government initially objected to UNESCO's decision to declare it a World Heritage Site.

The film graphically depicts the conditions in which Korean workers were kept. The brutality of the Japanese was such that it could not have been motivated solely by the desire to obtain the maximum of coal at a minimum of cost. After all, people do not work best when treated worst, though some bosses still appear to think so. At any rate, the film portrays the sadism of the overlords, which apparently is well and indisputably documented. Everyone accepts this, except perhaps the Japanese themselves who find it difficult to accept.[12]

As I watched scenes of the Japanese maltreat the Koreans with what seemed like joyful malignity, as a kind of patriotic duty, scenes that alas were all too believable, I could not but reflect on the strange disjunction between the Japanese whom I have known and this revolting conduct. On the one hand there is charm and the utmost delicacy, and on the other insatiable savagery. In like manner, the Japanese have the most refined aesthetic sense and a penchant for the sheerest kitsch. And indeed, one quite often hears the argument that, since people of refined civilization so easily turn to savagery, to be civilized in the sense of refinement of taste is morally useless. Were not the Germans the most cultivated people in Europe? This was the burden of argument of Professor John Cary, the distinguished literary critic, in his book, *What Good Are the Arts?* In this book, he demanded empirical evidence that cultivated people were morally superior to the uncultivated, and came to the conclusion that they were, if anything, worse. The word civilization now rarely appears without quotation marks. It is as if, by appreciating Utamaro or Hokusai, I make myself susceptible to commit Japanese-style atrocity.

---

[12] As do the people of most nations that have committed atrocities.

The action of the film takes place towards the end of the war when it is obvious to almost everyone that it is lost by the Japanese. Nevertheless, the war effort is continued, and the Koreans still abused. Many of the Koreans have been fooled into coming to Hashima: for example, one of the main characters called Lee, the Korean leader of a jazz band in Seoul (it had never occurred to me that there might be such a thing as a jazz band in Seoul in 1944), and his young daughter whom he has taught to sing and dance à la Shirley Temple, has been offered a job on Hashima. When he arrives, he is press-ganged into the mines and his daughter taken as a sexual slave.

The intrigue of the film is very complex and not always easy to follow. It involves the superficially civilized but utterly ruthless and cruel director of the mine, an apparent Korean nationalist leader who is actually a traitor, and Korean gang leaders. Although very anti-Japanese (it could hardly be otherwise), it does not portray all Koreans as square-jawed, iron-resolved heroes who are so united that they never quarrel among themselves, betray each other, or seek personal advantage at the expense of others. Lee is shown to be willing, and indeed eager, to cringe cravenly before the Japanese masters whenever it is in his interests, or those of his daughter, to do so. This is plausible: willingness to cringe before the powerful, especially when they have the power of life and death that they are prepared to use in the most casual or whimsical fashion, is a common if not admirable human trait. I do not know that in the right (or rather the wrong) circumstances that it would not be mine. I think most people, in searching their own biographies, would find instances in which they did not stand up for right, even when the consequences for them of doing so would have been far less serious than death.

In 1945, the island undergoes aerial bombardment by the Americans. It is clear that the end (of the war, not the film) is nigh. The Japanese know that the Germans are by now being tried for war crimes and some of them executed. The director of the mine and his deputy therefore try to destroy the records which show the large-scale exactions and cruelty to which they have been party and for which they will be held responsible.

Does this necessarily mean that they knew all along that what they were doing was wrong, that they felt guilty? After all, what would they have had to fear if what they had done was right? Did the destruction of the extermination camps before the arrival of the Russians, Americans and British mean that the Nazis knew that what they were doing was not only wrong, but wrong in a uniquely terrible way?

The answer is not straightforward. What the Japanese in the film knew was that the Americans would think that what they had done was inexcusably wrong, but that is not the same as thinking it wrong themselves. They knew that the Americans might punish them severely, even execute them, but they would think this merely victors' justice, no different morally from military defeat. They had nothing to reproach themselves for according to their scale of values. One of the Japanese in the film asks why the Koreans were not grateful to us, the Japanese, as if they, the Koreans, had been the beneficiaries of Japanese munificence (this might be called *the oppressors' delusion*).

The deputy director who takes over after the director has

been killed in a raid realises that the most incriminating document of all is the memory of the Korean workers, so that he decides to kill every last Korean on the island. The Koreans, getting wind of this, decide on a desperate plan of escape. They will overpower the Japanese and take the coaling boat that plies between the island and Nagasaki to Korea. There follows in the film a long sequence of the final battle between the Koreans and the Japanese that put me in mind of something I heard in my youth when I was an aficionado of Hammer horror films, namely that the studio made extra-bloody versions for the East Asian market. (I still do not know whether this was true; I suspect that it was not.)

Although the film claimed to be based on historical events, I found — on summary search — no record of an escape by Korean workers from Battleship Island. Even if there had been such an event, it still would have seemed to me that the prolonged battle scene at the end of the film was pruriently and gratuitously violent, more to indulge a taste for blood and possibly for vicarious revenge than for artistic purposes. Indeed, the whole film was explicit, and the problem with the explicit in film is that it turns everything into spectacle, whereas the implicit works by insinuation into the imagination:

> Tell all the truth but tell it slant –
> Success in Circuit lies...

Or, as the great psychologist and literary critic, Joseph Stalin, put it, one death is a tragedy, a million deaths is a statistic. No one knew this better than he.

The last scene of the film is a little troubling. The Koreans, after heavy losses, have taken control of the boat and are beginning to steam towards their homeland. As they do so, the second atom bomb ever used in anger is detonated over Nagasaki. The Koreans see the mushroom cloud rise, and they know the war is won. This is the first time I have ever seen a nuclear explosion taken as a symbol of liberation. One of the Koreans on the deck of the boat says (as the last line in the film), 'A lot of Koreans live in Nagasaki.'

This is both ambiguous and chilling. The moral arguments over the use of the bomb are well-known. In its defence is the supposition that, although the Japanese would have lost the war in the end, without the bomb they would have gone on fighting to the bitter end at a cost of millions of lives both American and Japanese. Against this it is asserted that the Japanese were on the verge of surrender anyway and the Americans knew this. The bomb was not used to defeat the Japanese but to warn the Soviets.

To decide between these arguments requires detailed knowledge that I do not have, and probably no evidence would be decisive or indisputable anyway. But the ambiguity of the words 'A lot of Koreans live in Nagasaki' would remain even if questions *were* settled once and for all. Do they mean that a special value is to be given to the lives of Koreans by comparison with the Japanese? That the Japanese deserved to die but not the Koreans? While all too understandable in the circumstances, is this way of thinking not what gives rise to the problem in the first place?

I remember the reply that Victor Gollancz gave to someone who said that the Germans, living in the most terrible circumstances in the immediate aftermath of the war, deserved the cold and starvation from which they were suffering.

'And the children?' asked Gollancz.

18

HOTEL SALVATION, DIR. SHUBHASHISH BHUTIANI, INDIA

If I had to choose anywhere to live but Europe or Australia, I think it would be India (provided I had at least some money). Indeed, when I was young, I had the fantasy of living the rest of my life in a simple lodging in India — in Patna, perhaps — contemplating existence and writing short stories of great economy and depth. Like most youthful fantasies, this one did not come to fulfilment, but *Hotel Salvation* revived it in me though, my days being past their best, I should no longer be prey to such illusory desires, even fleetingly.

In the film, a man whom I should once have called elderly but now seemed to me merely late-middle-aged, a widower who lives with his son, daughter-in-law and granddaughter, decides that his time has come, that is to say he is soon to die. We never discover how or why he has come to this conclusion, for he looks notably healthy, if we discount his being slightly overweight because of his good appetite. He proposes to go from the small town (small for India, that is), where his son has a job as a clerk in an insurance company, to Benares, the holy city on the Ganges. To be cremated there on the banks of the river is the best possible end to a Hindu's life.

In Benares there are hotels like the Hotel Salvation of the film's title that cater specifically to the needs of those who are dying and wish to die by the Ganges. These hotels take guests for two weeks only, at the end of which period the guests, if they have not died within the prescribed period, must leave and find lodgings elsewhere.

The son accompanies his father to Benares and lives with him in the hotel. The son's relations with his father have never been easy and the son is not a happy man in general, not with his work, not with his wife and not with his daughter, who not only does not want to marry the man selected for her but wants to go out to work. Moreover, she had been taught by her grandfather to ride a motor scooter, which (for her father) represents a scandalous degree of freedom or looseness for a young woman. He is a man disappointed in life.

Before father and son leave for Benares, a pandit comes to the house to conduct a ceremony to ensure a safe journey. It might seem strange to the supposedly rational western mind that anyone should attend a ceremony to wish him a safe journey to the place where he is to die soon after arrival, but I have long since come to the conclusion that there is an underlying wisdom to the apparent absurdities and contradictions of Indian life.

The pandit conducts his ceremony with a charming and pretty little holy calf. I have noticed that there seems to be very little laid-down procedure to the ceremonies that pandits conduct, and those who attend them seem also not to have much idea of what is going on or being said, certainly not in the way an observant Catholic, say, would follow a Mass. At the marriage of the son of an Indian friend of mine in

Calcutta, I asked my friend's brother what the Sanskrit prayers uttered by the pandit meant as he addressed a small fire which he fed with spices and sprinkled with water, to which my friend's brother replied, 'I don't know, it's all Greek to me.'

How very Indian! This mixture of perfect English humour (better than any now heard in England), mysticism and respect for ceremony for its own sake, is what I love in India. The contradictions living happily side by side, the archaic and the modern, without any attempt to reconcile them by means of an overarching theory, are to me delightful, a kind of instinctive wisdom.[13]

The taxi in which father and son travel caused me a pang of nostalgia: it is an old Ambassador car that, when I first went to India in 1969, and long afterwards, was the only model available.[14] I suppose that I should be against state-granted monopoly, as it tends to inefficiency and corruption, and yet I much preferred the Indian roads and traffic jams when all the cars were the same except for very minor variations as to

---

[13] A less happy example of this contradiction was in a notice I saw in Calcutta outside one of the new shopping malls to which the newly prosperous middle-class, in my view foolishly, resort (foolishly because everything in the bazaar is so much better and cheaper). 'Remember,' said the notice, 'it is illegal to selectively abort female foetuses.' More amusing is the Ballygunge Circular Road, where I stay when I am in Calcutta. It is a one-way street, but at 1pm the one-way changes direction. Somehow or other, in a very Indian way, the confusion caused by the changeover sorts itself out.

[14] It was based on a 1950s Morris design, long outmoded.

colour. Somehow this lessened the urban aesthetic disaster that is the motor car, though I must also admit that the Ambassador was not the most comfortable of vehicles and after a few years had a tendency to move slightly crabwise while bellowing like a wounded animal.

The landscape through which father and son pass is flat and dusty and not very beautiful, and yet with a powerful capacity to induce nostalgia in those who have known it.

Father and son duly arrive at the Hotel Salvation where they are greeted by the proprietor. Is he a holy man or a fraudulent businessman? Is his eye fixed on eternity or the main chance? One simply cannot tell, and in the end one does not care.

Of course, a form has to be filled on arrival. Does the old man, supposedly dying, suffer from diabetes? From epilepsy? What can any of this matter when he is to die within two weeks? But bureaucracy springs eternal.

They soon meet Vimla, a widow whose husband died in the hotel and whose room is decorated as if it were her home. They ask her whether she has arranged her room so elaborately to stay a mere two weeks. Vimla has lived in the hotel for eighteen years, not two weeks.

One's heart leaps for joy. Humanity has triumphed over the rules that humans have made and then bow down and worship. A human being has overcome regulation. How many of us deem ourselves free and yet are hemmed in at almost every moment of our lives by regulations of doubtful necessity?

The supposedly dying man and Vimla soon become close, but before long she does actually die. Perhaps the happiness of having formed a close connection with a man after eighteen years of widowhood makes it an appropriate time to die;[15] and then the relatively-old man follows suit (though he still has no discernible illness, other than a brief episode of fever from which he recovers). This is not quite as sentimental as it sounds because the timing of our deaths, even from natural causes, often has a psychological aspect. When one of a married couple dies, the other, if it has been a long marriage, often soon follows, or those who approach their hundredth birthday while ill postpone their deaths until they have reached it. Approaching Christmas has the same effect: such are our tiny victories over Death, otherwise always victorious.

Just before he dies, the father sends his son home: he wants to die alone. By now their relations are somewhat mended, the 'difficulties' having been far more on the son's side than the father's. The father's desire to die alone, which is directed against no one and is not intended as a commentary on any of his relations, is rather a wise acceptance of death and the limits of human existence which most of us, having neither religious belief nor any apprehension of the tragic dimension of life, never achieve. The supposed right to health, frequently advocated, makes of death an infringement of rights; but while individuals' deaths may be unjust, Death itself cannot be.

The interiors shown in this film, though simple, are of great beauty. They are like still lifes, almost painterly in quality. The Hotel Salvation is not luxurious in any ordinary sense, or even

---

[15] Now more than ever seems it rich to die,
To cease upon the midnight with no pain...
— Keats, *Ode to a Nightingale*

comfortable, indeed I suspect that to many it might appear horribly or intolerably run-down. There is no laundry service, everyone must prepare his own food, fetch his own water, or at least arrange for these things to be done. But for me, at least, there is another kind of luxury at the Hotel Salvation: freedom from possessions. Pascal said that many of the problems of the world were caused by our inability to sit quietly in a room: to which we might add that much unhappiness derives from our inability to do without possessions (much easier in a tropical climate, of course).

To many it will seem strange that the Ganges — a muddy brown river, after all, the colour of tea with milk — should be regarded as holy. (At the beginning of the film, the son's boss, when informed that his father intends to go to Benares to die and he wants to accompany him, asks whether it was the Ganges that made Benares holy, or the other way round.) All I can say, feebly, is that the Ganges has a certain *je ne sais quoi*, though whether I should have felt this if I had not known of its unique status, I do not know.

There are anti-religious rationalists in India, but somehow their objections to ancient traditions and ceremonies on rational grounds seem thin, like the tinkling of a triangle without an orchestra. There were many things in this film that appeared irrational: for example, the father's belief that he was soon to die though he was not ill, the belief that the banks of the Ganges was the best place to die, the rules of the hotel that in fact were no rules at all. But to quote Pascal once more, the heart has its reasons that reason knows not of. All is not rational that is rationalist. If I could choose a place to die, it would be on the banks of the Ganges.

19

LA RÉVOLUTION SILENCIEUSE, DIR. LARS KRAUME, EAST GERMANY

I have lived (though strictly by choice) several years under authoritarian regimes, and being by nature timid, obedient and conventional, I was not much bothered by them. They were not totalitarian, however, and I think that the distinction between authoritarian and totalitarian regimes is a valid one, though no doubt, as with all human phenomena, there are intermediate and marginal forms.

The main difference — the difference that makes modern totalitarian regimes so much less bearable than authoritarian ones — is that, while under authoritarian rule there are things you must not say, under totalitarian rule there are things that you must say. You must assent to, applaud and repeat things that you know to be false: and, from the point of view of the rulers, the more false they are, the more obviously at variance with the most evident reality and lived experience, the better, for the greater the disparity between what is known to be the case and what must be uttered, the more thoroughly is the probity and self-respect of individuals destroyed, and the greater their humiliation in the face of power. A humiliated population without personal probity is docile and easy to control. Oddly enough, the totalitarian technique of humiliating people by making them intone absurd falsehoods which they cannot possibly believe to be true has become ever more widespread in all kinds of organizations, public and private, since the downfall of the Soviet Union, as if in effect the latter had won the Cold War, at least in cultural effect, instead of having lost it.

What is also remarkable, considering the importance of the totalitarian experience in the Twentieth Century, is how comparatively few films explore it imaginatively by comparison with other forms of oppression. Perhaps this is because intellectuals in general (and film-makers are intellectuals, at least where they have at least *some* artistic pretensions) have a bad conscience with regard to totalitarianism, many of them having been indulgent to, if not downright supportive of, it, especially in its communist incarnation. But this German film, *The Silent Revolution*, without resort to cheap caricature, does explore the East German experience of communist totalitarianism, without the slightest indulgence towards it but also without salacious lingering over its most brutal or bloodthirsty aspects. The makers have understood that it is always best to leave something to the viewers' imagination.

The story of the film is said to be a true one, but this always leaves one wondering precisely how much of it is true. After a lapse of more than sixty years (the time when the action takes place), how much of the dialogue can be true to what was actually said? The majority of the actors in the film (above a certain age, of course) were born and grew up in East Germany, an experience which gives at least plausibility to their performances. But plausibility is not accuracy. Nevertheless, I was (as ever) willing to suspend my critical faculties for the duration of the film.

The Silent Revolution tells the story of a class of Gymnasium pupils in East Germany in 1956 who were about to take their *Abitur*, the qualifying examination for admission to university. They are, by definition, an elite: they are bound for the upper echelons of East German society, such as it is. They are not deeply rebellious by nature and indeed by today's standards are deeply respectful of their elders in their day-to-day behaviour. But though they believe, *grosso modo*, in the benefits of socialism as they have been taught them, they have lively and enquiring minds, and so do not believe everything they are told simply because they are told it. In 1956 East Berliners could still, under certain conditions, go to West Berlin, whose freedom and increasing prosperity they could hardly fail to notice by comparison with the constant drabness around them.

News of the Hungarian uprising or revolution, and of its bloody suppression by the Soviets, filters through to the class. Some of the class listen clandestinely to West Berlin Radio (a crime in East Germany) in the isolated house of an old intellectual homosexual who has a radio that can receive the station. It relays the false news that the great Hungarian footballer, Ferenc Puskas, has been killed in the suppression of the uprising.

The class decides to hold a one-minute silence in honour of Puskas just before a history lesson. This small act of rebellion has ever-increasing consequences for these young people on the verge of adulthood. The ripples are like those of a stone thrown into a pond, spreading outwards, except that they grow ever stronger as they spread.

It is a virtue of the film that the history teacher in whose class the original tiny act of rebellion takes place, and the headmaster of the *Gymnasium*, are not portrayed as tyrannous monsters, but rather as ordinary decent human beings who are trying to do the best they can in the difficult circumstances. They try to keep knowledge of the rebellion confined to the school in order to protect the pupils from the consequences, but they do not succeed. In a totalitarian state, nothing can be kept hidden and even the tiniest manifestation of dissent, *a fortiori* collective dissent, is a serious matter — control being all or nothing for totalitarians. A local school supervisor, charged with finding the instigator, takes over. She is intelligent, vicious, ruthless and determined. Her method is essentially that of blackmail: she has the power to ruin the lives not only of the pupils themselves, but of their parents. In a totalitarian state, everyone has something to hide from the authorities which can be used as a lever to his destruction, and it is the duty, and probably the pleasure also, of the secret police to know what that something is, to be held in reserve until it becomes most useful.

Eventually, even the Minister of Education is involved. He arrives at the school in his large black Soviet limousine with white-walled tyres. In him, ideology has replaced all human feeling. There is a terrible sincerity in him (we often forget that sincerity may be a vice worse in its effects than cynicism). An old communist, he was tortured under the Nazis and uses this experience as a moral justification for his own ruthlessness, a moral justification that assumes that there are only two alternatives for Man in the world, Nazism (evil), and Communism (good), and that therefore everything to further or consolidate the latter is itself good, indeed *the* good.

The children — or adolescents, or young adults — decide between them what to say. Some of them are for telling the truth, that their minute's silence was in solidarity with the Hungarians, but others think it better to pretend that they were mourning the death of Puskas and nothing more. Taking a vote, they decide on the latter story. A great deal, they now realise, is at stake for them. If they are not permitted to remain at the *Gymnasium*, if they are not permitted to take their *Abitur*, they are destined for factory work and, all the communist guff about the dictatorship of the proletariat notwithstanding, to be a factory-worker in East Germany in 1956 was an unenviable fate. In fact, far from being a dictatorship of the proletariat, East Germany is a dictatorship of the *petit bourgeois* apparatchik bureaucrat class: that is, if one is obliged to talk of classes.

The lie that they were merely mourning the death of Puskas, however, reveals that one or all of them must have been listening to West Berlin Radio, for it is only by that means that they could have learnt of it. More and more psychological pressure is applied to them to reveal who their ringleader is, but in the end, after many twists and turns of the screw, they manage to stick together. Thirteen of the sixteen of them manage to escape to West Berlin, where they take their *Abitur* successfully, but at the cost (they suppose at the time) of never seeing their parents again. This is a terrible price to pay, for they love their parents; and indeed, one of them decides not to leave with the others because he thinks his two younger brothers will miss him too much. Thus, he is condemned by his love for them to another thirty-five years of life in a totalitarian state — a state which, moreover, must have seemed at the time likely to endure for ever. Thus, the ending of the film is happy but unhappy, or unhappy but happy. It is excellent that the thirteen escape to freedom, but it is sad that freedom should be so tinged with sorrow, a sorrow that can be put to the back of the mind but never altogether forgotten.

The Silent Revolution had a special resonance for me for more than one reason. A close friend of mine, who alas died recently, escaped from East Germany two or three years after the events portrayed in the film, being at the time a year older than the protagonists. His grandfather, an anti-Nazi, had spent time in Buchenwald, the concentration camp. He became the headmaster of a school in Weimar after the war but was anti-Russian in his sympathies and walked a very hazardous tightrope. He could not have been unlike the headmaster in the film.

My friend never saw his parents or grandparents again after he left East Germany (he had resisted learning Russian, which in the circumstances of the time amounted to rebellion) and did not feel safe to return until the fall of the Berlin Wall, by which time they had died.

He never spoke, except in the most general terms, of his time in East Germany. Aged eight at the end of the war, he must surely have lived through a great deal, of an intensity that must have made everything after his escape seem peaceful but pallid. He never spoke ill of anyone, at least of anyone in particular. Even of the Nazis and Communists, and those who believed in Nazism and Communism, he would say only that they were mad, ill in the head; for him it was the only possible explanation of their faith in doctrines at once so terrible and so stupid.

I never asked him about his experiences and of course cannot do so now. His childhood experiences, unlike mine, must have been of historical interest.[16] I felt instinctively that his way of dealing with his past — not the same as forgetting it — was not to talk about it, and I respected this. For me to have enquired after it, as I often wanted to do, would be to have destroyed peace of mind for the sake of more or less idle curiosity. Just as there are thoughts that lie too deep for tears, so there are experiences too painful to be dwelt upon.

We live in times in which there is a prejudice in favour of talking, as if talking were necessarily curative of pain. Those who do not talk of what they have suffered are deemed to have committed treason against themselves. If you say of someone that he doesn't want to talk about it, it is usually in a tone of accusation. He *should* want to talk about it; he is morally deficient.

I do not believe this. My mother, too, was a refugee from Germany, who arrived in England in 1939 aged 19. She, too, never saw her parents again. They were not killed, but managed, two or three months before the outbreak of war, to escape to China. My mother was to join them there but by then it was too late, too dangerous, to do so.

---

[16] Happy the land whose children have no experience of historical events.

My mother never spoke of her experiences, and I felt intuitively that I should not ask her about them. It was up to her to speak of them if she so wished. When, having previously resolved never to set foot in Germany again, the Mayor of Berlin invited her to Berlin on the sixtieth anniversary of her departure, she decided to go — but unaccompanied by me. This I understood. One does not search for one's ghosts even with people closest to one. In the event all she recalled was the street plan of her home area, the buildings having been destroyed. Perhaps this was just as well for her.

I understand the impulse not to talk: muteness seems to me a perfectly reasonable (if not invariably beneficial) response to experiences that shake the soul. This is not at all to say that the experiences should be forgotten. A film like *The Silent Revolution* performs a valuable service in allowing us to enter imaginatively into the experience of totalitarianism: an experience whose horror we are in danger, such is the shallowness of our contemporary culture, of forgetting only thirty years after it ended, thanks in small part to the understandable unwillingness of those who experienced it *in propria persona* to talk about it.[17]

---

[17] Many in East Germany had much to hide, as the opening of the *Stasi* files revealed.

20

14 POMMES, DIR. SHISI KE PING GUO, BURMA

When I think of Burma, I experience a pang of guilt. I was fortunate enough to go when it was an all but forbidden land to foreigners, when none but diplomats were allowed to stay longer than a week. It was a military dictatorship, the corrupt, brutal, superstitious and mendacious General Ne Win being still the *éminence grise* of the regime. As was by then usual in Burma, civil war was raging, as it had more or less continuously since independence (under the name of the *Union of Burma*). The economy, under what the regime itself called 'military socialism,' was not thriving, to say the least. No development whatever had taken place for several decades. Everything was run down; the latest cars (and there were few enough of *them*) were from the early 1950s. Their side windows were often of plywood, and they had to be coaxed into activity, like aged, half-starved beasts. The buildings, none new, were crumbling. The roads were so potholed that the potholes seemed like traps for cars. There was an air in the country not of perpetual motion, as in some South East Asian countries nearby, but of perpetual immobility. It felt as if this is how it had always been and how it would always be.

There was no freedom as usually understood: all opposition was ruthlessly suppressed. Any political gathering was broken up, often with great violence. Official propaganda extolled the present situation as if it were the acme of human achievement. It was tyranny tempered by laziness and incompetence. It was xenophobic and self-serving, and I ought to have hated it.

Instead, I loved it. The country had an indefinable charm that any modernisation would destroy once and for all; the charm was as delicate and irrecoverable as the blush of a grape. I looked at the country aesthetically, not politically or economically. No doubt this was very superficial: people do not live in museums for the delectation of occasional visitors. I have little doubt that if I had had to live there, I would have detested the government and done what little I could to rid the country of it. But still I could not be as enthusiastic as I ought to have been about the prospect of democratic change.

What would such change bring? First it would bring international-style architecture to destroy all sense of place, turning Rangoon into a minor Bangkok. It would bring shopping malls and the shallow pleasures of consumerism. It would bring fake Versace sunglasses, fake Gucci toilet bags (neither of them wonderful even in the original) and traffic jams. It would be another step in the destruction of difference, no doubt accompanied by hosannas to the virtues of diversity. I could continue with my bilious diatribe against the most hideous aspects of the modern world that democracy would bring in its wake, forgetting that modernity had allowed an ever-greater proportion of the people of the world to live in at least a degree of comfort.

The first scene of the film confirmed my worst fears. It takes place in a market in Mandalay over which loom tower blocks indistinguishable from those of Birmingham or Manchester. In the Mandalay of my day, nearer forty than thirty years ago, there were no such buildings. Here, then, was progress.

The protagonist is some kind of businessman (a type that once hardly existed in Burma) whose business is not doing well and who, as a consequence, suffers from insomnia and other symptoms of anxiety. At his mother's request he consults a fortune-teller who tells him to spend two weeks as a monk in a remote Buddhist monastery, taking with him fourteen apples to eat (hence the title of the film), one a day for the duration of his stay. The first scene is of him buying the fourteen apples in the street market.

The woman at the market stall offers him three kinds of apples, imported from China, Thailand or California. This in itself symbolises the opening of Burma to the world, for during the prolonged period of military socialism the country claimed to be all but autarkic, smuggling being the only source of foreign goods. (In my time, the visitor had on entry to the country to register any possessions such as cameras or watches, to ensure that he took them with him when he left and did not sell them in the interim.)

Having selected his apples with care — he buys the Chinese, though told the Californian are the best, again symbolic of something — he sets off for the monastery. His car is right-hand drive though Burma decided to change to driving on the right- rather than the left-hand side of the road, though its two neighbours, India and Thailand, drive on the left. The change was supposedly symbolically anti-colonial, since both the British and the Japanese also drove on the left, and was typical of the useless, costly and time-consuming measures taken by unpopular bureaucracies to avert ideological criticism by semi-intellectuals, and to distract attention from their own corruption and incompetence. Change is a substitute for improvement. I saw the same phenomenon many times in British hospital administration, so perhaps the phenomenon is another manifestation of modernity.

The protagonist drives for a time on the type of road that didn't exist in the Burma of my day, traffic jams as yet not having caught up with the road improvement, but soon turns off on to an unpaved track that in the monsoon season would be impassable. In the dry season it is merely rutted and dusty, and he passes through villages where the habitations are still of straw. Not far short of his destination, his car gets stuck in a dried riverbed, and the local village children, in return for a packet of biscuits (a treat for them, for they live almost outside the money economy), push him out. But though the village is almost outside the money economy, I noticed that baseball caps have reached even here, another sign of democratisation, and I recalled a travel writer, whose name I forget, whose ambition it was to reach places on the earth where Nescafé had not reached.

The monastery was far from all that I had imagined. Here was no stupa covered in gold, no reclining Buddha of enormous size, nothing but a single-storey wooden building elevated slightly above the ground, no doubt to protect it from monsoon floods and cobras. (I read somewhere that there are 3000 deaths from snakebite a year in Burma.)

The new and temporary monk is shorn immediately of his

hair, as used to be those who entered prison, a symbol of retreat from the world and its usual preoccupations. But what is surprising in the subsequent sequences is the almost complete absence in the monastery of any life that could be called spiritual. There is no reading or recitation of the scriptures in which Buddhism is so rich, as I had expected there to be. There is no meditation, but on the contrary a seemingly banal day-to-day existence. There are no ceremonies, no chanting, no incense, no wind-chimes or prayer wheels, none of the appurtenances we associate with Buddhist temples and monasteries, even (or perhaps especially) those in suburban London. It is all rather disappointing.

The main activity of the businessman-turned-novice-monk, now dressed in his purple robes, seems to be the collection of alms for the monastery from the local population. It is astonishing to see the reverence in which he is held just because his hair has been shorn and he now wears purple when only shortly before he had been a sleepless, failing businessman with no particular acquaintance (as far as one knows) with Buddhist doctrine or ceremony. He is now called *master*, and everyone — or perhaps I should say every woman and every girl — prostrates herself before him, prostration in the most literal sense. One is reminded of *The Captain of Köpenick*, the play in which a man in Wilhelmine Germany extracts obedience merely by donning an army captain's uniform. My individualist and rationalist self experienced a slight frisson of disdain at this Burmese willingness to bow down before mere symbols such as a shaven head and a purple robe so uncritically, all the more so as the monastery seemed to be purely parasitic, bringing nothing in the way of practical charity or spiritual consolation to the local population it parasitized. The monastery's main concern, as depicted here, is with getting enough to eat, and in so far as it offers instruction to child monks (in Burma and elsewhere it is an honour for boys to spend some time as novices), it is to instil superstition into them, such as it brings bad luck to touch women's clothes that have just been washed. Of Buddhist philosophy, which is admirable even when one thinks it mistaken, there is no hint.

The local women bring water to the monastery and empty it into the water-tank so that the monks may wash. There is a long and seemingly dull sequence in which the camera follows a procession of village women with pitchers on their heads trudging from the river to the monastery, but the length of the sequence does succeed in conveying the arduousness of the task. The irreverent thought comes to the modern western mind: why can't the monks, who spend most of their time doing nothing and just sitting around, fetch their own bloody water? Are the local people, or rather women, nothing but unpaid servants of the monks? And is my reaction the one that the film-maker intended to arouse in viewers?

There is, of course, the question of the veracity or verisimilitude of the film. I know from personal experience that editors of films and soundtracks can, with editing, change the whole meaning of what one says, can make the heroic seem cowardly, the compassionate seem unfeeling, and so forth. Did the makers of the film start out with the desire to make monastic life appear meaningless and parasitic, perhaps from the village-atheist point of view? (The film, I noticed at the end, was Chinese, though with much Burmese participation.) Buddhist monks have often formed a dangerous political opposition for lack of any other, protected as they are from naked suppression to some extent by their supposed spiritual authority. In other words, the film may be propagandistic, though I admit this is mere uninformed speculation.

Nothing, indeed, would be easier than by careful selection to make the life of monks appear vacuous or worse. While most of us do useful work some of the time, none of us does useful work all of the time, and it is in the nature of human existence that much of it should be banal, because life makes banal demands on us. In other words, in watching a film such as *14 Pommes* we are entirely at the mercy of the honesty and judgment (or otherwise) of the film-maker. If he has in this case rigorously excluded all that is spiritual in the monks' lives, of course nothing will be left but the quotidian and the seemingly parasitic. Nor do we have any way of knowing whether this monastery is unique or typical. Without much more detailed knowledge than most of us possess, we can have no idea whether we are being manipulated or informed.

But let us suppose for a moment that the monastery and its monks are as parasitic and useless (pragmatically) as the film appears to make out. Would it then follow that they serve no purpose? I think not. Although I am no believer myself in any religious doctrines[18] I have long since expunged from my heart the adolescent Voltairean inclination to mock, and I return to

---

[18] Whether Buddhism is a religion is, of course, a matter of dispute.

such mockery only if someone tries to force his beliefs upon me or pursues some evil in their name. I know that people can and do derive great consolation from doctrines that do not appear well-founded to me, but which of us can say that our own source of consolation (life being such that we all need one) is entirely rational? Would the life of the impoverished Burmese be better if they were disabused of the piety? What would, or will, replace it?

My view of Burma is incurably romantic and one-sided, if not a quarter-sided or an eighth-sided:

> For the temple-bells are callin' and it it's there that I would be –
> By the old Moulmein Pagoda lookin' lazy at the sea…

And this is so even though an angry saffron-robed monk, near the Shwe Dagon Pagoda in Rangoon, approached me and set about me with his black umbrella, shouting 'Get out of Burma! Get out of Burma!'

I sympathised with him. Too many people like me would ruin it, as they are probably ruining it even now. Burma is one of the countries that you leave but that never quite leaves you.

21

FRONTIÈRES, DIR. APOLLINE TRAORÉ, WEST AFRICA

How could I resist a film that followed several market women in their journey across West Africa by bus? I had made a similar journey myself a third of a century before, though of the countries passed through by the women — Senegal, Mali, Burkina Faso, Benin and Nigeria — I had passed though only Mali and Nigeria. All the same, the division of the countries being to a large extent an arbitrary imposition, I recognised a great deal.

Some things had changed in the meantime. The buses in which the market women travelled were far more comfortable than any in which I had travelled. They were larger and luxurious by comparison, the number of passengers equalling the number of seats (except when an enormously fat woman took two). In my time, seats were not assigned to passengers, nor was there any system of booking places. You simply turned up at the bus station, usually a dusty space with a goat tethered to a tree, and found a bus (sometimes with difficulty) that was going to your destination. There was no timetable either, but your bus left only when nothing more — animal, vegetable or mineral — could be squeezed into it. You travelled with cargo and contraband, goats and chickens, babies and bicycles, with baggage tied and boys clinging to the roof, the sides of the bus hung with goods like ripe fruit from a tree. It was astonishing how much a small bus could take, though it subsequently moved only under protest, gears clashing and engine grinding. 'When are we going?' I would ask the driver or his assistant of uncertain but important duties. 'When we are full,' he would reply. 'But you are already full,' I said. Little did I know. The word 'full' as applied to buses in Africa meant something completely different from what it meant in Europe.

In *Frontières*, by contrast, which I take, I hope correctly, to be an accurate reflection of the situation today, there was none of this former chaos, so irritating but also so profoundly human. If the conditions of bus transport are anything to go by, West Africa has prospered by comparison with thirty years ago — unless, that is, bus passengers are members of an elite, like owners of private jets among us. But the roads, too, are much better, suggesting at least some general material progress.

Some things don't seem to have changed very much, however, among them the exactions of soldiers, police, customs and immigration officers at borders between countries, even those that supposedly have free movement between them. The worst border I experienced was between Niger and Mali, especially on the Malian side. There it took three days to go a hundred yards. All the passengers (except me) were arrested three times by different groups of officials, customs, police and army, and those who resisted payment were imprisoned overnight until they coughed up the next morning, having previously sworn that, having already paid so much at other borders, they had nothing left. I was excluded from this extortion, but I had to sleep by the side of the road those nights. Everyone was very polite to me: 'This does not concern you, monsieur,' said the various officials. I found it agreeable to sleep under the stars in the clear, semi-desert air, but by the end of the third day I had grown a little exasperated and went down the road (only a short way) shouting, '*Pots de vin! Pots de vin! Post de vin!*' (Bribes! Bribes! Bribes!), whereupon a soldier calmed me down. He said, 'What you have to remember, monsieur, is that we haven't been paid for three months.' It was a good lesson in moral relativism.

Sometimes I would turn up at a border unexpectedly, on my own, and tourists were not very frequent thereabouts, to put it mildly. The border guards would keep me waiting for hours, though I was the only person waiting to cross and they had nothing else to do. They would either go to sleep or pretend to be very busy. Obviously, they were expecting me to offer a bribe but this, being still something of a purist or puritan in these matters, I refused to do. I had a copy of *Moby Dick* with me, one of those many books that one feels one ought to have read and is glad once one has read it, but to whose pages (at least in my case) one does not turn to with a song in one's heart. Being stuck between the border of Gabon and Equatorial Guinea, however, is the perfect occasion for reading it, for it is more amusing than doing nothing. It has the merit, for these purposes, of being very long, and the perfect instrument for a duel of wills between a corrupt border official and a priggish traveller. *Moby Dick* helped me through more than one border without having paid a bribe.

In this film, the border guards and officials in uniform were far more menacing than I remember them as having been. The difference is explicable in more than one way.

The first is that, any improvement in the standard of living notwithstanding, the officials actually *are* more menacing than they were. There is now more for them to steal, and it has to be remembered that I passed through none of the borders depicted here, where local tensions might have been high.[19] It is possible that my presence as the only white man altered the conduct of the officials since, as they say in parts of Africa, the death of one white man will give you more trouble than the deaths of a thousand black men. In crossing Africa from Zanzibar to Timbuktu by public transport, I met nothing but courtesy and kindness.

It was possible too that in those days I was still naïve and, still thinking well of the world, missed the menace, the threats and violence that were present under my very nose. I certainly saw none of the sexual violence or exploitation that this film graphically depicts, which varied from sex as a bribe to officialdom to outright rape by officialdom. In all my months of African adventure, I never felt the slightest tremor of fear, but that might have been as much due to the insensitivity of my antennae as to any absence of threat. For example, I went through Rwanda finding it, by comparison with most African countries, well-ordered, clean and efficiently run only a few

---

[19] It never crossed my mind, for example, that Mali might erupt into Islamist violence.

years before one of the most thorough genocides in human history was to take place there. I passed though North-West Nigeria sublimely unaware of the Moslem fundamentalist movement that was brewing or in preparation. In Kaduna and Maiduguri, I felt perfectly safe and bought Hausa robes for myself to the delight (or was it mockery?) of the local merchants. They said that it showed that I liked the people — which I did. It is true that in Sokoto there had been a recent confrontation between the Christian community and the Moslem over the right to drink alcohol, but it never occurred to me that this might be the harbinger of something much more serious. Indeed, personal security in the Moslem part of Nigeria was far more assured than in the Christian south, no doubt partly for a rather simple reason. While I was in Sokoto market, a young thief was caught and nearly beaten to death by an angry mob. I learnt that the police, however, rented out their guns at night to robbers, the police and the robbers having found a *modus vivendi*.

In the film, as I have said, the women suffer far worse than anything I witnessed, but as I now realise, I was far too superficial an observer. I did not enquire of my fellow-passengers what had happened or been done to them during their nights of imprisonment, and I assumed that it was only money that officialdom was after. How naive I was!

The women passengers in the film, all on their way to Nigeria for business purposes or to attend a wedding in Lagos, help each other in various ways to dodge the exploitation to which they are all subjected. They resort to various subterfuges to which I had been witness, and which are made necessary by the conditions of African life. As the Nigerian journalist, Peter Enahoro, once said, there is no such thing as an honest Nigerian. An honest Nigerian would either soon die of hunger or cease to be an honest Nigerian.

Halfway through their journey, the passengers on the bus see the horrible consequences of a motor accident. In Africa, such accidents seem to occur for no obvious reason, though they are often attributed to black magic. Once in Tanzania I passed the scene in which a mother and her five children were killed. The mother and children were laid out in descending size on the side of the road like the pipes of an organ. Apart from being a little dusty, they looked unharmed. They had crushed or suffocated to death under the sacks of maize on which they were perched when the army lorry on which they had hitched a lift failed to make it up a hill and started to slide downwards. The mother and children slid off, followed by the sacks of maize. The sight is with me still.

My medical assistant, Christopher, a very intelligent young man, said it must be an evil spirit that caused the accident because so many accidents occurred on that hill. I gave a somewhat less fatalistic explanation. If you overload vehicles and do not maintain them properly, for example by attention to brakes, such accidents will happen. Yes, said Christopher, but not all the vehicles involved in accidents on that hill were overloaded, so why did they happen there? Careless driving, drunkenness, speeding, I suggested: there was more than one possible cause of accident. Yes, but why *there*? A drunken driver wasn't drunk only on the hill. There must be an evil spirit dwelling there.

Later in the film's journey the women's bus, now in Nigeria, is attacked by armed robbers, the leader of whom speaks as if he has been much influenced by American black gangster culture (I use the word 'culture' in its anthropological sense, that is to say the sum of all human activity that is not merely instinctual). One of the women refuses to part with her valuables, another pushes the robber-chief so that he falls flat on the ground. He shoots her dead for this act of *lèse-majesté*, and the robbers then flee. This act of violence is credible and its consequences deeply affecting. One had grown to like the victim, a forceful woman. Nothing makes one appreciate the value of the life of a human as the wanton taking of it.

When I was young, I braved journeys with a high chance of being killed, I suppose to prove to myself the value of life. Once I went on the bus from Mbabane in Swaziland to Maputo in Mozambique. It was during the time of the RENAMO insurrection, and their guerrillas had intercepted the previous bus on this route and hacked everyone on it to death with machetes. I found the journey exciting, every yard of it an escape from death. I think that if I had seen this film beforehand, I might have chosen an alternative mode of transport.

One aspect of this film particularly pleased me and brought back happy memories. Many of the market women were very fat, but the way in which they dressed and carried themselves, with colourful robes and splendid turbans, gave them a dignity and even a magnificence that was a joy to behold. They were quite unlike the slovenly obese of our latitudes.

My late friend, Peter Bauer, a very distinguished development economist, had nothing but respect for these market women, who often carried with them large sums of cash, carried out complex calculations in their head, invested with shrewdness and prudence, and whose word was their bond.[20] If he had seen this film, he would not have changed his opinion.

[20] He had made a detailed empirical study of market relations in Nigeria in the late 1940s.

22

UNE ANNÉE POLAIRE, DIR. SAMUEL COLLARDEY, GREENLAND

The frozen north has never much appealed to me. Its beauty, however great, seems to me limited and, dare I say it, cold; its flora and fauna are exiguous and its population scarce, so that it lacks the immediate interest of other climes. This is all prejudice, of course, and many sensible and sensitive people have felt differently. There is a whole genre of literature, much of it fine, devoted to polar exploration.

Of Greenland I know practically nothing. What I know could be contained in a single shortish paragraph. I know it is very large, especially on the Mercator projection; it is a Danish possession, now semi-autonomous, though how and when it became Danish I do not know; it is the subject of a bad poem, *Greenland's Icy Mountains*; in the Thirteenth Century, or thereabouts, its climate was considerably more hospitable than it is now, when food could be grown there, a possibility that may now be returning; its centre is covered in ice thousands of feet thick; and those whom I grew up calling Eskimos without any derogatory connotation, and whom I must now call Inuit, live there. There are polar bears in Greenland, and seals and whales in the seas around. I think of igloos and blubber when (as happens rarely) I think of Greenland. It is becoming a tourist destination for those whose geographical palates are jaded by too easy accessibility to the *hoi polloi*. *Voilà* the extent of my knowledge of Greenland.

This remarkable semi-documentary is about a young Danish teacher who chooses to go to a village on the east coast of Greenland, which is remote even by Greenland's standards of remoteness, which are high. He is told at his interview for the job that it is unnecessary to learn the local language because it is his job to teach the local children Danish — or how else will they join the modern world? At first, he follows this advice, but he soon finds that all he has to teach is of no interest to his young pupils. How can they possibly be interested in the history of Martin Luther (Lutheranism being Denmark's state religion) when they have never been outside their hamlet of eighty souls? Anders, the teacher, comes to realise the absurdity of what he has been sent to do.

When he tries to teach the children according to the Danish school curriculum they misbehave, pay no attention, mock him and learn nothing. Only when he tries to incorporate himself into their way of life do they come to respect him. He learns how to drive a husky sled, to fish through a hole in the ice, and so forth. And the children are much more interested in learning these skills themselves than in matters utter alien to their way of life and environment, whose meaning they cannot begin to guess.

Ardent pedagogues might draw a general conclusion from this (perhaps they are intended to do so): the doctrine of the need for education to be relevant to the lives of the children to be educated. In the West, at least, this seems to me a dangerous and reactionary doctrine. I do not suppose that anyone would deny the necessity for teachers to engage children's interest, but the situation of children in a hamlet on the east coast of Greenland is hardly typical of that of the world's children as a whole. It is, or should be, one of the goals of education to broaden a child's notions of what might be relevant to him. The purpose of education is not to enclose children in a cultural laager, irrespective of what that laager contains. This is not to deny that good or inspiring traditions should be overthrown or not passed down merely by teaching a passing acquaintance with other traditions: there is a balance to be stuck. But much of education should be *irrelevant* to children's lives rather than relevant: or else, what is the need or point of it?

Anders comes from a farming family. The farm has been in the family for eight generations and he, an only child, wants to break with that tradition, destiny or fate. This, surely, is symbolic of a great change in western society, now almost defined by its individualism: the increase in the importance of personal desire by comparison with continuity of a way of life. But is it not slightly odd, then, that Anders should ardently desire the preservation of a tradition not his own, as if other traditions were, almost *ex officio*, superior to the one he has left behind? This is the mirror-image of colonialism, where colonialism, when it is not merely depredation, conceives of itself as having a civilizing mission. Anders, then, is a symbol, whether he knows it or not, for good or evil, of the European loss of self-confidence. Where such loss leads to genuine self-examination and hesitation in imposing oneself on others in the name of civilization or any other ideal, it is all to the good, but when it goes too far, it becomes self-lacerating, frequently somewhat dishonest (in that self-hate comes full circle to self-love) and even suicidal.

Traditions are not preserved in aspic or as flies in amber. They persist but with an admixture from outside themselves; the village to which Anders goes is clearly an example of this. At the end of the film, in which the characters, except for him, are played by the villagers themselves, Anders remains the teacher, but teaching in schools can hardly be an immemorial tradition among the Inuit. The people no longer dress in sealskins or use whalebone harpoons. Their boats are mainly modern, with outboard motors. Even their kayaks are the product of modern industry. Their homes are lit and heated by electricity; they have framed photos of relatives on their shelves, and we even see children eating bread, hardly a traditional item of the Inuit diet. Their fishing hooks are of steel and their fishing lines of nylon. I could continue indefinitely, but the point is made: the Inuit, even here, are not untouched by modernity.

Indeed, it is worth noting that they are, in fact, Lutherans. When an old man dies, the grandfather of a village boy, Asser, to whom Anders has become particularly attached though at first Asser was hostile and refractory, he is first buried in a coffin (not made of local materials) in the snow, and then, when the winter gives way to the brief summer, when the land is covered in tough grass and wild flowers, he is re-interred in the village cemetery according to Lutheran rites, which apparently reflect the sincere beliefs of the villagers.

Still, the ability to fish though the ice and manage husky dog sleds (albeit not of local manufacture), to subsist on a diet of fish and seal-meat, and to know the local legends, are a justified source of local pride and self-respect. Before Asser's grandfather dies, he teaches Asser the skills that he himself learnt as a young man or boy, for example how to make a leather harness for a husky. One cannot but regret the wholesale loss of skills in our societies, our reliance on others for practically everything.

The scenery (and photography) of the film is magnificent, of a beauty to which only clichés can do justice. The deep blue of the sea, the pure white of the mountains, the radiance of the lighter blue of the sky, are such as to induce an almost mystical state of ecstasy. Here is the world before Man got his dirty paws on it and besmirched so much of its surface for ever (though it must be admitted that many of the landscapes we think of as of natural beauty, for example those of the English countryside, are really a co-operative effort of Man and Nature). Another mystical moment is when we — and Anders — see the Northern Lights, the Aurora Borealis. You immediately think that this is something you must see before you die, or else you have missed one of the glories of life. It is a sight of which you could never tire, like music by Bach.

The central episode of the film is a journey by sled into the interior by some of the male villagers, in which both Anders and the young Asser take part. It is a cliché to say that the scenery is to take one's breath away, but this is no more than the literal truth, though it is also frightening in its sublimity. How small is Man, how insignificant, how overwhelmingly powerful are the forces of nature, and how utterly indifferent to his fate! A terrifying wind suddenly blows a snowstorm down from a mountain on to them and threatens to engulf them, but the villagers know how to construct an igloo in no time and take shelter in it snugly. By contrast, the dogs, for whom one cannot but feel a profound admiration, remain outside, but come to no harm because of their thick coats. These dogs are infinitely willing, give or take a necessary crack of the whip, and even seem quite content with their lives. There is no place for sentimentality in the relationship between man and dog in this environment, however. There seems to be none of the individual relationship which is the joy of the urban dog-lover.

By the morning the storm has passed, the skies are blue, and the sleeping humans are woken by the frantic barking of the dogs. This can mean only one thing, the presence nearby of a polar bear. It is a polar bear that the villagers have been hunting, and the previous day they had caught sight of his paw-prints in the snow, so that they know he must be near. And in fact, as they emerge from the igloo, they see the bear at a distance of a couple of hundred yards, a magnificent creature, but a female with two young cubs. Because of the cubs, they decide not to shoot her — with a gun, not a traditional weapon.

If the bear had been a solitary male and they had shot it, would the film have shown the scene? One can imagine all too easily the bear's bright red blood spreading through the pristine white of the snow, a sight to horrify the over-refined such as we. Such is the salience of polar bears in our minds that the film-maker would probably not have dared to include it, for it would have destroyed the message of his film. We think of polar bears as soft toys, not as apex predators; and who can tolerate cruelty to soft toys?

Our attitude to polar bears has not always been so indulgent, to say the least. Not long ago I reviewed an excellent and handsome book by an American writer and aficionado of northern wildernesses on the history of our attitudes to the polar bear.[21] At one time they were regarded as a ferocious and dangerous enemy, a pest, almost to be stamped out wherever encountered. The world did not always hold its breath over the fate of a polar bear cub in a German zoo, as it did recently. The change in attitude is perhaps due to a guilty loss of contact with Nature in the raw. Nature is no longer an enemy that has to be battled against so that it may yield up a living; it is, rather, a benevolent goddess whose sanctuary, the earth, we profane.

The film does show some dead seals, other creatures that, because of their whiskers and appealing eyes and faces, stimulate our affection, and even on two occasions dead seals being skinned by villagers. But the actual means by which they were killed is not shown, for fear of losing the audience's sympathy.

How odd we are! If we were to see people killing hyenas we should not feel in the least upset. On the contrary, we should feel that the hyenas got what they deserved, though they couldn't help being hyenas. A hyena is not called a hyena for nothing.

---

[21] Ice Bear, Michael Engelhard, University of Washington Press, 2016.

23

LA MAUVAISE RÉPUTATION, DIR. IRAM HAQ, NORWAY

The bad reputation to which the title of this film refers is that of a young girl of Pakistani descent whose parents have emigrated to Norway. Her father's ideas of correct behaviour remain those with which he arrived; but his daughter, having been brought up in Norway, has very different ideas. This results in a conflict between them of a type with which I was very familiar from my work in a British hospital in which I had as patients many young women of Pakistani origin brought up in Britain. The film by no means exaggerates the violence of the cultural and generational conflict, or the depth of the tragedies in which it often results. Terrible as is the situation depicted in the film, I have known worse.

The father in the film is in some ways an enlightened and even admirable man. To have emigrated from Pakistan and to have achieved modest prosperity by owning and working long hours in a shop in so alien a land is a small triumph of the human spirit. To cross half the world in order to offer a better future for his family takes courage and determination.

Nor is the father a religious fanatic. Indeed, there is no religious reference in the film at all, though whether this is for prudential reasons one does not know. No one prays or offers a religious justification for his conduct. In the home there are, it is true, kitsch depictions of Mecca that I saw in most of the Moslem homes in Britain that I visited, but there are no citations of the Koran on the wall. The father's ambitions are purely secular: he hopes that his daughter will become a doctor. The film thus implicitly denies that the oppression of women that it exposes is Islamic in inspiration or origin. Again, whether this denial is from prudence or conviction, I cannot say.

The girl, Nisha, goes to school where she is attracted to a young Norwegian boy. One day, he climbs into her bedroom from the balcony of the family's flat. Her father, Mirza, catches them there together and starts to beat the boy severely, stopping only when the neighbours call the police who then intervene. Although the film makes no mention of it, the fact that Mirza is not prosecuted and faces no legal consequences of his clearly excessive violence is surely significant. It is unlikely that, had he been of the white lower class and behaved in this way, he would have got off so lightly. Multiculturalism meets moral cowardice.

After this episode, Nisha takes herself to a shelter run by social services for abused women. An attempted reconciliation with her father, mediated by two social workers whose attitude of complacent bourgeois reasonableness is very well captured, breaks down when Nisha refuses to marry the boy with whom she has been caught because she no longer loves him. In my experience of such situations, Mirza's demand that she marry him because of the otherwise defiling physical contact that has occurred between them (they were kissing) is unrealistic. No father of Mirza's type, however partially enlightened, would make such a demand; a marriage with a white boy would itself be dishonouring, shameful, and Mirza is Islamic enough to have required Nisha to marry a Moslem. Nisha's refusal, however, provokes a terrifying outburst of Mirza's temper in front of the social workers, and the scene, while sociologically very unlikely, is dramatically effective.

What *is* realistically portrayed is Nisha's loneliness and feelings of isolation in the women's refuge. She is, after all, still very young; she has hitherto lived in a very close family that provides warmth and support in return for strict adherence to its constricting norms. When, during a telephone call to her mother, she is offered a return home and a new start, she joyfully (and naively) accepts. This is also realistic, and not only for young women of Pakistani origin: it is a matter of frustration to doctors and social workers that abused women often return to their abusers merely on the strength of an easily given assurance of reform.

In the meantime, Mirza has consulted with other men of Pakistani origin living nearby. They have persuaded him that he must do something about Mirza's behaviour, both for the sake of the family's own reputation which has been sullied and for that of the whole community (as any group with characteristics in common is called these days). If Nisha gets away with it, her kind of conduct and independence of mind, her participation in the easy and, it must be admitted, not altogether attractive ways of western youth, will spread and become general. Mirza has a duty to the community.

Again, from my experience, this strikes me as very realistic. Men of Pakistani origin in England, even a generation or two removed from Pakistan, were 'protective' of their daughters and sisters, and reacted with violence when the system of relations was threatened by female insubordination. They instinctively understood that this system was all-or-nothing, hence the ferocity with which they defended it. Nisha's tragedy is that she is caught between two worlds, being fully at home in neither.

When Mirza and his son Asif come to the refuge to take Nisha home, she soon realises that she is not going home. Instead, they drive her to the airport. This again is very realistic. Many of my young patients had been taken to the airport and flown 'home' to Pakistan, either to marry against their will (usually an older first cousin in their ancestral village whom they had never seen before, and who often spoke no English) or to put them back on the straight and narrow path of subordination to the men of the family, as often as not a life of domestic service plus sexual servitude, in complete disregard of their personal wishes or inclinations. This is so common a pattern that, inside the women's lavatory doors in Birmingham airport are affixed notices informing those who are being taken away against their will that they can call the airport police to rescue them. This escape route, of course, can easily be closed by the confiscation of the young women's mobile phones (as their passports are confiscated, except when shown to border officials). I suspect that the notices are there not to help the women but to prove that the authorities are doing all that they can. Be that as it may, we see Mirza snatching Nisha's telephone and throw it out of the car window *en route* to the airport.

Mirza warns Nisha not to make trouble at the airport by

letting anyone know that she is not travelling by her own choice. As soon as they arrive in Pakistan, they travel to the town from which Mirza emigrated physically if not mentally. In contrast to most of the cases with which I was familiar, Mirza's family is both urban and middle class, and far from living in abject poverty, they seem to live at a standard of living in some ways higher than that of Mirza and Nisha back in Norway. Not only their standard but their mode of living is not unattractive. The maker of the film is presumably anxious to escape clichés.

Mirza leaves Nisha in the care and control of his sister and brother-in-law, who burn her passport.[22] Nisha's life is now circumscribed by an endless round of domestic tasks (and gossip) in which she is expected to participate, which she finds boring and knows is intended by her father as her destiny for the rest of her life.

She falls in love with a handsome cousin of hers who

---

[22] In one case known to me, a man took his family — his wife and daughters — 'back' to Pakistan, where he destroyed their passports. His wife was in a wheelchair because of her Parkinson's disease caused by his constant beating of her about the head. He thought that without their passports they would be stranded in their remote village in Pakistan, leaving him free to live with another woman back in England as he wished, without the inconvenience of having to pay for the upkeep of his family. One of his daughters, however, more resourceful than he imagined, managed to contact the British consul who, familiar with this kind of problem, had them returned to Britain. As Gerard Manley Hopkins put it (though with something different in mind), 'No worst, there is none.' Indeed, I could tell a story even worse or more tragic than this.

reciprocates her love. They meet surreptitiously and escape into the town one evening. They snatch a few moments of happiness together but are caught in the act of kissing in a doorway in a dark alleyway by three patrolling policemen who beat the cousin, strip Nisha and make them perform sex acts together which they film on their smartphones. They return the pair of them to Nisha's family, where Nisha is now virtually locked up as a prisoner and has the reputation of being a complete slut, having twice been caught *in flagrante*. The police, of course, take the opportunity for blackmail.

Mirza is recalled from Europe to arrange matters. The solution for him is obvious: Nisha should marry her cousin. But because of her reputation, the cousin's parents will not hear of it, and the boy is too obedient to his parents' wishes to go against them, though his feelings towards Nisha were real enough.

Mirza then removes Nisha from his family. *En route* in the countryside, he stops the car and walks her to a precipice from which he orders her to throw herself. She pleads with him, and for a time we fear that he will push her over to an inevitable death, but in the end, his love for her (which is real) wins the conflict with the bubble, reputation. He takes her back with him to Norway.

There Nisha resumes her schooling but under conditions of family surveillance as strict as surveillance in North Korea. Either her father or her brother waits for her at the school gate; she is never allowed out on her own. Finally, her parents find her a potential husband, a Pakistani doctor in Canada whom she meets for the first and only time via Skype. She is told that, he being a doctor, she will never have to work. She agrees to marry him, and family relations seem to have been restored, but soon afterwards she escapes (via the balcony) from the flat in the middle of the night. From the window of the flat, her father sees her running down the lamplit road. He could run after her and no doubt catch her, but he does not do so. Perhaps he has learned his lesson, or perhaps he merely recognises defeat. There is the same ambiguity as in the ending of the Iranian film.

The film is a powerful portrayal of the conflict between two cultures in the heart of one family. It is not quite as simple as a conflict between men and women, though the conflict has a far worse effect on the lives of women than on those of men. Women who grow up in, and accept or do not question, the traditional role assigned to them by their culture are not necessarily wretched, and indeed often do their best to preserve it in the next generation. They are as appalled by rebellious young women as are the fathers. They are oppressors as well as oppressed — if, at least, the whole situation is to be described as one of oppression.

But, at least in my opinion, the film depicts not so much raw injustice or oppression as the tragedy of misunderstanding. (We are, of course, averse to the notion of tragedy these days.) Mirza is not a monster, even though he nearly kills his own daughter; on the contrary, he is a good man caught up in a situation in which powerful emotions conflict for him irresolvably. He tells Nisha early on, in an attempt to get her to see 'reason', that he has sacrificed a great deal so that she should have a better life than his, and this is no more than the truth. He loves his daughter too; he believes (as surely all responsible parents must sometimes do with their children) that his refusal to let her go her own way is for her own good. He has not the imagination, as most of us do not, to realise that, when it comes to the fundamental questions of human existence, there can be opinions other than his own.

He is also a racist. He has nothing but contempt for the people to whose country he has emigrated. Like most people, it does not occur to him to wonder why the better life that he seeks (admittedly in merely material terms) should be found in the West. For him, economic prosperity has no intellectual, philosophical or spiritual roots. It is no more to be wondered at than Norway's cold weather, which is a fact of nature. Moreover, his concept of morality is almost entirely a question of shame, and boils down to what the neighbours will think, there being no appeal to individual conscience or judgment. Tradition and custom alone are the arbiters of right and wrong.

And in truth, the culture to which Nisha wishes to flee is, in its most superficial but increasingly prevalent aspects, far from an attractive one, but on the contrary crude and debased. At the beginning of the film we catch a glimpse of Nisha in a night-club, so called, where youth are as conformist as in any mosque. Who could say that a little more sense of shame and decorum, without making it the whole basis of morality as Mirza does, might not do us good?

A Bad Reputation is not a sensationalist exaggeration of the misery brought about by a clash of incompatible conceptions of life; on the contrary, it deepens our understanding of it. By comparison with the fathers and brothers I saw in my practice, Mirza is sophisticated and flexible. The brothers were anxious that their sisters should be obedient to their fathers' command because they, the brothers, wanted the system, by which they could have the best of both worlds, to continue: a compliant wife at home and participation in the Sodom and Gomorrah of British life outside. They could have their cake and eat it. Every girl I met in Nisha's situation knew of other girls who had been killed for refusing their fathers' orders, to preserve family honour. They were taken to their ancestral village and, if still refractory after a little imprisonment or physical abuse, killed. It cost £5, I was told, to pay off the police afterwards.

24

DOMINGO, DIR. FELLIPE BARBOSA, BRAZIL

Domingo is a kind of Brazilian *Cherry Orchard*, with the charm of the latter's characters deliberately omitted. The action takes place, as in the *Cherry Orchard*, in a country house, to which the owner, who lives mainly in the local metropolis, Porto Alegre[23], has returned for the fifteenth birthday of her granddaughter, who lives there with her son and well-hated daughter-in-law. There is to be a grand party for the local bourgeoisie; most of the action of the film takes place immediately before it, at precisely the moment that President Lula is inaugurated after his election.

The parallels with the *Cherry Orchard* are considerable, and (therefore) so are the contrasts. Both take place at a time of tremendous social change and upheaval. In the *Cherry Orchard* the inheritors of the old landowning class are about to lose their land through their fecklessness, a fecklessness that is the consequence of an outmoded sense of entitlement that renders them incapable of adjustment to the new, more meritocratic

---

[23] Rather than Paris, from which Madame Ranevskaya returns.

world. The son of one of their own former serfs, who by hard work and intelligence has taken advantage of the new opportunities, is about to buy the estate to which his father and grandfather were once tied; there is thus a poetic justice in this but also tragedy, in that the new master, by his dynamic entrepreneurialism, will destroy the beauty and charm of the place. There is loss in the gain: improvement is not a straightforward ascent.[24] The losers in the historical process are worthy of our sympathy even as we recognise their faults, and may have qualities, such as refinement, generosity and absence of crude materialism, that are attractive.

We do not get any feeling of this in *Domingo*, rather the reverse. The assumption of power by Lula is felt by the upper-class in Brazil to be a threat to its existence (in the event, it was no such thing), but we are led to feel no regret at its possible passing. This is because, in the film, it has no charm and no taste or refinement. Its pleasures and desires are simply those of the lower classes writ large, like those, shall we say, who win the lottery. They are as feckless as Madame Ranevskaya but without the charm or the generosity. They cannot even be bothered to dress elegantly: except for a moment of ostentation at the party with which the film ends — during which, symbolic of its incompetence and unworthiness to rule, there is a power cut — it dresses in a way indistinguishable from the inhabitants of the *favelas*. It has no virtues, only vices, and the most common ones at that. Even in the pursuit of love

---

[24] This shows Chekhov's largeness of mind. His grandfather bought his release from serfdom only 19 years before Chekhov was born.

affairs it is crude; it does not have any of the reticencies or ambiguities of the *Cherry Orchard*, nor any sense of melancholy or nostalgia, let alone tragedy. For them there is only sexual frustration, no chagrin d'amour. Even its manner of eating is without refinement, as if it were but the satisfaction of a biological necessity carried to the point of self-indulgence.

The charm of the declining aristocracy in the *Cherry Orchard* is accompanied by a deep egotism, of course. When everyone else has left the mansion, the ancient retainer, Firs, is left behind. Although he has faithfully served the family all his life and made that faithful service his entire purpose of existence, they forget him at the last as if he had been but a piece of movable furniture. 'Life has slipped by as though I hadn't lived,' he says, lying down after the departure of the others. Chekhov leaves it uncertain whether he will ever get up again.

There is no such ambiguity in *Domingo*. The old servant of the family who has killed, skinned and butchered a sheep for the family party is himself killed — electrocuted — when he tries to pull the trip-switch after a power cut. His death appears not to affect the family at all; life has slipped him by as well, as though he hadn't lived. In effect, he is killed by the family's negligence in not maintaining the house properly, but no one feels guilt or even regret. For them, he is utterly expendable.

In the *Cherry Orchard*, another servant, Dunyasha, drops and breaks a saucer. The representative of the soon-to-be dispossessed family, Varya, reacts simply by saying, 'Well, that brings good luck' — foolish if believed, perhaps, but kindly. But when the servant in *Domingo* breaks one of the champagne glasses that the matriarch has brought to the party, a violent scene ensues. The contrast in attitude to material objects is striking: on the one hand indifference (perhaps of a lordly kind), as being unimportant, and on the other a vital importance as a symbol of wealth, status and control, as if power grew out of the bowl of a champagne glass. In the first case is an inherited certainty of social superiority and therefore of no need to display it, in the second an awareness of the fragility of the claim to high position (the inauguration of President Lula, watched nervously on the television, being a manifestation of the fear of the poor's revenge). The Russian aristocracy in decline is much more attractive that the Brazilian bourgeoise in decline, or at least in anticipated decline.

Is that bourgeoisie as gross and unattractive as here depicted? The bourgeoise of any country has never been the favourite social class of artists or intellectuals (has it ever been romanticised, except to a very slight extent by Karl Marx?). No artist or intellectual has ever gained much cachet by openly preferring the bourgeoisie to the proletariat, though he usually prefers a bourgeois income to a proletarian one. If proletarians have faults, they can usually be explained away by their circumstances; but no such indulgence is extended to the bourgeoisie who are bad because the bourgeoisie, *ex officio*, is bad of its own free will and choice.

But in fact, members of the Brazilian bourgeoisie whom I know, admittedly intellectuals or of intellectual bent, and not at all representative, are not at all as those in the film. On the contrary, they are often far more cultivated than their counterparts in Europe or America, perhaps because of a sense of cultural inferiority that they must somehow make up for. They feel they must prove themselves, in a way that those who have inherited a grander cultural tradition, who feel cultivated by virtue of the accident of their place of birth, so to speak, do not.

Strangely enough, however, members of the Brazilian bourgeoisie to whom I have spoken have precisely the same opinion of their own class as that suggested in *Domingo*. For them, their own class was worthless, parasitic, without virtue or charm. For them, the rich were heartless and vulgar, concerned only to preserve their own privilege, increase their wealth and indulge in the most conspicuous consumption possible. They did not even perform one of the most important functions and justifications for the existence of the rich, namely the creation of a legacy of beauty for future generations. In Brazil they were neither charitable nor did they create anything like the magnificent cultural institutions of the United States. They were wholly selfish and served no larger purpose at all.[25]

Unlike so much of the self-abasement that one encounters among the intelligentsia of the more metropolitan countries, which strikes me as often exhibitionist (I am unworthier, and therefore better, than thou), the self-denigration of members of the Brazilian bourgeoisie seems to me genuine and deeply-felt, and therefore not complacent. I think that many Brazilian bourgeois (or at least the ones I have met, including students) feel a genuine sense of shame that their class has contributed,

---

[25] I note, however, that the finest collection of European art in the Southern hemisphere is in Sao Paulo.

and continues to contribute, so little to their country and to the world's store of art and science.

At the end of the film, the family holds a (relatively) glittering ball, in which they finally take the trouble to dress properly, for the rich of the locality. It is for the 'coming-out' of the matriarch's granddaughter. But by then we have witnessed all manner of sordid goings-on in the family, for example the attempt by the birthday girl's brother, who had just reached the age of puberty, to assault a servant girl sexually. In other words, the ball is but a veneer and the underlying reality is not at all elegant, by no means an original theme.

Certainly the ball does nothing to redeem the moral squalor and physical slovenliness of all that has gone before. The glitter is that of a fish rotting by moonlight. But if one is forever digging down to the rotten foundations of elegant structures, of exposing the sordid realities behind beautiful facades, will one end by seeing nothing beautiful at all in anything? One will look at a picture of a servant girl by Chardin and say, 'Yes, but the life expectancy at the time was less than thirty.'

I am, within reason, in favour of veneer and appearance, provided they are of the right sort. I do not look at an elegantly attired old lady and think how shrivelled and ugly she must be in a state of undress.

25

RETABLO, DIR. ÁLVARO DELGADO-APARICIO, PERU

The *retablo*, or retable, of the title is a little painted box whose doors or flaps open on to a brightly painted biblical (or less frequently an historical) scene of figures made of dried and hardened potato paste. Such *retablos* are a folk-art of the Ayacucho region of Peru, attractive and joyful to the eye.

I bought one of these *retablos* twenty-seven years ago during the electoral campaign that brought Francisco Fujimori to power. ('Why did you vote for him?' a reporter asked a peasant. 'Because I know nothing about him,' replied the peasant. This implicit attitude to the political class of his country is now shared by electorates around the world, the Peruvian peasant was a prophet.) It was the time when the Maoist, or Pol-Potist, revolutionary movement, *Sendero Luminoso* (Shining Path) was at its apogee and it seemed far from impossible that it would topple the government. Interestingly, the *retablo* tradition was adapted, or adopted, by *Sendero*, such that the Holy Family was replaced by Presidente Gonzalo, the founder, leader, and ideological guide of the movement, who was the object of a personality cult at once repellent and ludicrous, the angels in the new iconography

189

being the guerrilla fighters. Gonzalo was the *nom de massacre* of Abimael Guzmán, who was, before he assumed for himself the mantle of the Messiah of world revolution, professor of philosophy at Ayacucho University.

But the world and Peru have moved on since those days (fortunately enough), indelible as they are in my memory. The story of *Retablo* is simple enough. The action takes place in a village in the bleak mountains around Ayacucho, where an artisan who makes *retablos* for sale in the city tries to pass on his skill to his only child, a son. He is known as one of the best artisans in the field and has agreements to supply both the church and rich Peruvians with examples of his work. Father, son and mother (who has a stick because she limps from foot-drop, probably from polio) live an apparently simple and harmonious life in a typical local house.

The son admires the father and tries to learn his craft. The father teaches him how to model and paint the figures or figurines. The relations between father and son are affectionate. (The dialogue is mainly in Quechua.)

One day, father and son go together to deliver a particularly elaborate *retablo* to a magnificent colonial church. They have no vehicle or animal of their own and at first transport the *retablo* by human porterage — their own — until they hitch a lift in a passing pick-up truck. The son, Segundo, sits in the back with the *retablo*, the father with the driver in the cab.

It is on this journey that Segundo sees his father masturbating the driver though the cab's back window. Unsurprisingly, this disturbs him profoundly. From being a quiet, obedient and well-behaved son, he changes into one who is aggressively taciturn and fractious. Suddenly, without saying why, he refuses to work any longer in his father's workshop.

His mother, always something of an authoritarian, tries to find out the reason for the change in her son's behaviour, but he will not tell her. Then, a little while later, Segundo returns home to find his mother tending his father who has been very savagely beaten, nearly to death in fact. His mother sends Segundo to seek help from the local village headsman, who has a reputation as a healer. This is a part that ambulances do not reach.

When Segundo reaches the headsman's house, the latter refuses to help. He says that he will not help a man like Segundo's father. It is clear that the villagers have learned that he is a homosexual (or more strictly a bisexual), and it is they who have administered the beating.

When his wife also learns of it, she resolves at once to leave him. She begs Segundo to come with her, but Segundo asks who will then look after his father, who is far from recovered. Segundo resolves to stay, and we see his mother limping away, goodness knows to what life.

Segundo pays for the sins of his father. When he tries to carry one of the remaining *retablos* that his father has made to the city to sell (his wife having gone into his workshop and smashed most of them in a fit of vengeful rage), he is intercepted by a gang of local boys who self-righteously tar him with the same brush as his father. They taunt him until Segundo retaliates; a fight ensues from which Segundo rather implausibly emerges victorious.

His father gradually recovers but advises Segundo to re-join his mother, who was unsurprisingly devastated by his decision to stay with his father. Still Segundo refuses: despite all, he plans to take up making *retablos* again with his father. When his father protests that no one will buy them because of his reputation, Segundo suggests that they move to somewhere that they are not known.

The father does not agree to this. One morning, overcome by shame, guilt and the need to liberate his son from his contaminating existence, he sneaks out of the house and throws himself down, or hangs himself in, the family well.

Next, we see Segundo making a *retablo* of his own to place in his father's coffin. Segundo speaks to his deceased father and tells him that he will remain in his heart forever. The final scene shows Segundo wrapping the tools of his trade in the kind of blanket that South American Indians use to carry their possessions, and then setting off from the house, whither neither he nor we know. To search for his mother? It is doubtful, though not explicitly ruled out.

Being a doctor, I am probably excessively literal-minded, but I was a little disturbed by the manipulative implausibility of some aspects of the ending. Of course, the film is fiction, not documentary, and therefore must be granted poetic licence, but it is also a work of social realism, so it ought to be minimally realistic.

Did the father kill himself by hanging or by throwing himself down the well? We briefly see Segundo climbing into the well, but either way he must surely have experienced great difficulty in recovering his father's body. As it happens, I have once in my career had to catch a man as he threw himself over the ledge of a roof three storeys up; I had him by one arm while a hospital porter had him by the other. Between us we had enough difficulty in not dropping him, let alone in hauling him up to safety, which we should not have been able to do but for the fortuitous arrival of two policemen on the scene. 'Let me go, you bastards!' shouted the man, followed immediately by 'Help, I'm falling!' Consistency is a rare characteristic of men.

Segundo must have been very busy after he recovered his father's body, for he not only made a rather neat coffin and dressed him in his best clothes but made and painted a special *retablo* to inter with him, and all this before he showed any signs of decomposition. There was no sign of asphyxiation or injury; on the contrary, his face would have made any mortician proud, so tranquil and perfect did it now appear. Segundo would also have had to dig the grave — all without local assistance, for the theme, the whole message, of the film is that prejudice destroys human sympathy and solidarity. But how could Segundo have achieved all this in the time allowed by the film?

Does implausibility, anachronism or impossibility matter in fiction? I still cannot make up my mind on this matter, and certainly the emotional impact of the film is considerable.

My wife, who saw the film with me and lived for a year in a remote Andean village learning to weave à la Inca before resuming a medical career, did not remember any scenes of violence comparable to those (quite frequent) in the film. But, of course, there are many possible explanations of the disjunction between the film and her memories. She might have forgotten; she might not have noticed; her presence might have changed the villagers' demeanour; her village was nearer Titicaca than Ayacucho, and it is a condescending error to suppose that all groups of Amerindians are identical in their culture. Moreover, things might have changed in the intervening forty years. I seem to remember that the introduction of television or video into places that previously did not have it is followed a few years later (when children who had been exposed to it from an early age reach the age of adolescence) by a sharp rise in violence.

One thing that struck me about the fights between young men as depicted in the film, however, was that they were conducted according to certain informal rules or a code of honour, despite the viciousness of the disputes which preceded them. When Segundo fights the youths who taunt him, the fight is man to man; one of the taunting youths attacks him, not all of them at the same time, as if the attacking youth were the champion or representative of the rest. The others do not intervene even when Segundo pounds him in the face with his fists (how severely is implied by the fact that he, Segundo, has to bathe his fists afterward). The others could easily have prevailed over Segundo by numbers alone but refrain from doing so. This suggests something interesting: that no matter how high passions may rise, rule-bound behaviour persists, or at least *can* persist. Being in a passion, then, does not exonerate us from our bad behaviour, for it is rarely that *all* control is lost.

One other aspect of the ending of this film worried me, at least if I am right in thinking that Segundo was *not* going to return to his mother: namely the scant sympathy or understanding it extends to her. True enough, the prejudice of the villagers who nearly kill Segundo's father and ultimately cause him to kill himself[26] are powerfully depicted as unthinking and cruel. But what of the mother's unenviable situation? For all her faults, she tried to be a good wife and mother, and her life is turned upside down through no fault of her own. By the end of the film, she is merely forgotten. Is pity not to be extended with those who cannot, at one gulp, accept a new morality?

Drama that campaigns for moral reform — and this I take *Retablo* to be doing — is necessarily one-sided. In Ibsen's *A Doll's House*, Nora leaves the Helmer household which she understandably finds stifling. Clearly, we are intended to sympathise with her or take her part, and because of Ibsen's brilliance as a dramatist forget entirely that, in so doing, she is abandoning entirely her three children. Is there not something chilling about this, when you come to think of it? Thus, needing one's space (as Nora needed hers) has become a need whose satisfaction trumps all others. The ego has landed.

---

[26] Removing himself from the world in this way might have been the only way he could think of freeing his son of stigma and was thus what has been called an altruistic rather than egoistic suicide.

26

UNE AFFAIRE DE FAMILLE, DIR. HIROKAZU KORE-EDA, JAPAN

A film may alter one's preconceptions of a country of which one knows little or nothing. I saw a Bhutanese film, for example, imagining Bhutan to have been a hermetic Buddhist kingdom virtually isolated from the rest of the world, its people leading a simple but meditative life, only to discover that mobile telephone signals penetrated even its remote forests, that its police were corrupt and its people avid for money. Despite my disbelief in Utopias, I had fallen prey — at least if the film depicted Bhutan and its people with a degree of accuracy — to the notion, assiduously peddled in our newspapers and magazines, of the real existence of a Shangri-La.

My view of Japan is largely a romantic one, a world of the refined aesthetic of Utamaro, Hokusai and Hiroshiga, among others. I imagine its population to be similarly refined, having mastered the art of living in a confined space with elegance. Though I know of the Yakuza, its crime syndicates, I imagine the country to be otherwise universally law-abiding (the Japanese football fans, after all, astounded the Russians when they cleared up after themselves after a match in a stadium in southern Russia during the World Cup, and the Japanese team left its dressing room cleaner than they had found it). Theft is so uncommon that the Japanese do not lock the doors of their houses; the streets of the city are entirely safe and no one so much as drops litter.

Of course, I know that this arcadian picture, however justified *grosso modo*, must be partial; and this film, *A Family Affair*, certainly filled in a few gaps. It portrays a society that is by no means immune from the social pathology with which we have all grown so familiar in the West and which for many years, as both doctor and writer, provided me with so much of my living.

The family of the title is anything but a normal one (if so proteiform an institution as the family can ever be said, on close examination, to be normal). In the film one meets a Japan that is far from the simple-minded model of industrial efficiency and personal compliance with social norms.

The family is not really a family at all. It lives in a little house that is scarcely bigger than a shack in a *bidonville*. The physical chaos inside is equal to that of any slum-dwelling in the West: so much for the hereditary, almost genetic, ability of the Japanese to beautify and make the most of a tiny space in which to live.

The two children in the family, Shota a young boy and Juri, renamed Rin, an even younger girl, are all but foundlings. Shota was left abandoned by his parents in a car, while Juri was taken into this recomposed family when she was similarly abandoned by abusive parents who beat her. Watching the film was a little like being back in the English hospital in which I worked for many years.

The Shibato 'family' is composed of members who have no family relationships, in the normal biological sense, to one another. They have come together for various reasons, and though they live in poverty and squalor, they are far from unhappy. The ancient matriarch, if such she can be called, has a small pension. When she dies, they bury her in the house surreptitiously, not wishing to draw the attention of the authorities to her death both because they want to continue to draw her pension and because they want to continue to live under the radar, as it were.

The man of the household, Osamu, having been injured at work as a day labourer, has become a professional shoplifter; he goes to 'work' with Shota almost as if shoplifting were a regular form of employment (I recall a case on which I was asked to give an expert opinion in which one of the witnesses, a heroin addict, said, 'We went out to work that morning', that is to say left the house with her fellow-addicts to go shoplifting in the next town, returning home at five in the afternoon, the day's work done). And although Juri, or Rin, is only five years old, she is taught to shoplift as soon as she becomes a member of the family.

Nobuyo, Osamu's wife, works in a large laundry where she steals all that she finds in the pockets of the clothes sent there to be cleaned. The brief glimpse that we have of this laundry suggests that not everything in Japan is modern or automated; rather, the laundry resembles a sweatshop *circa* 1914. Nobuyo has actually killed her first, abusive husband but has never been charged with this crime.

Aki (another member of the household or family) is a younger woman who believes that the old lady took her in out of sympathy for her predicament, having left her abusive family, but in fact only because she receives regular payments from Aki's father, who is the old lady's husband's son by a second marriage (it is all very complicated, as are the family relationships in British slums, where uncles may be younger than their nephews and nieces older than their sisters). Aki lives as a kind of prostitute, but a prostitute for a virtual age. Along with a troupe of other young women, she exhibits herself on camera while men at a distance choose one with whom they wish to speak. Somehow this seems worse than prostitution of the old-fashioned, *Maison Tellier* kind, indicative of a society in which experience is increasingly at one or more remove from material reality, and in which frustration must therefore be rife.

We see this very peculiar family take a trip to the seaside. Here they appear as happy as any other family on a day trip. We might be led to think that such a family represented as good a social arrangement as is possible, the idol of the normal family having long been shown to have feet of clay. But, in fact, it is all about to fall apart.

One day Osuma, accompanied by Shota, indulges in a new genre of crime (new for them, that is): he smashes a car window and snatches a bag that is lying on the back seat. By doing this, he reveals to Shota that his previous justification for theft is a sham, namely that while the goods remain on the supermarket shelf, they belong to no one, or at least to no individual, and that therefore there is no one who is hurt or harmed by shoplifting. The smashing of the car window is different, and Shota, though still young, begins to have qualms about what he and Rin have been doing.

Soon afterwards Shota deliberately sabotages a shoplifting expedition with Rin. He makes it obvious to supermarket employees that he is stealing. He runs away and they run after him. As they are about to catch him, he jumps over the wall or barrier of an overpass to the ground below where he breaks his leg. He is taken to hospital and soon his whole way of life becomes clear to the authorities.

Although Rin has enjoyed a better life with her adoptive (and adopted) family than she had with her real family, she has, from the legal point of view, been kidnapped. Osuma's argument that, since they never demanded a ransom, she couldn't have been kidnapped, is not accepted by the authorities and Juri (her original name) is returned to her real parents who, for purely public consumption, appear loving and respectable.

The body of the old lady buried under the house is discovered and Nobuyo takes all the blame and is sentenced to prison for five years. Shota realises that his so-called family were prepared to leave him to his fate in an attempt to escape or exculpate themselves, and sees that Osuma, whom he had come to accept almost as a father, has betrayed him. He is sent to an orphanage — Japanese social workers having been presented in this film, no doubt without intention to do so, as more intelligent, more compassionate and far better-dressed than their western counterparts.

As for Juri, the last scene makes it clear that her real family has resorted to type and is as abusive to her as ever.

What is the moral or meaning of this film, that was universally praised by the critics? It is (at least in my opinion) somewhat ambiguous, a little like life itself.

Much of the critical praise of the film employed the word *subversive*. It seems that subversion is to the literary arts what transgression is to the plastic ones, the highest possible achievement, irrespective of what is being subverted or transgressed.

But it ought to require very little reflection to realise that the quality of being subversive or transgressive cannot possibly be positive irrespective of everything else. For example, a subversive scientific idea, that triple immunisation of children causes autism, may result in tangible harm. Heresy is not an automatic corrective to orthodoxy.

What exactly, then, does this film subvert if it is believed to be subversive? Subversion can be deliberate or unintended, indeed it can be the very opposite of what is intended. I do not know what the director's idea was in making the film (he also wrote the script), but he was taken by the critics to be trying — and succeeding — to undermine both bourgeois propriety with regard to ideas of property, of the very notion of *meum* and *tuum*, and also of the proper constitution of the nuclear family. But irrespective of the director's intentions, which a film can in any case escape, I do not think this interpretation is quite valid. There is no story, as there is no experience or historical event, from which the wrong moral cannot be drawn.

Let us examine the question of theft. There is no doubt that thieves may form merry bands and take pleasure in their acquisitions that mere work would never have supplied them with. Transgression of the law or the rules can add pleasure to an activity, as every naughty child knows. Indeed, we might think that there is something wrong with a child who is *never* naughty: a lack of spirit, perhaps.

But the very possibility of naughtiness presupposes the existence of a set of rules to be broken. In a completely anarchic world, there could be no rules to break. And naughtiness becomes less attractive with age. If everyone did what he thought he could get away with, the resultant society would be very unpleasant. Universal naughtiness would soon bring forth universal surveillance, retribution and violence.

The conditions necessary to justify stealing are first necessity and second an inability to satisfy necessity by any other means, for example by work. These conditions can hardly be said to obtain in the case of Osuma and the adult members of his 'family'. Osuma was badly treated (we are led to infer) after his accident at work which rendered him for a time incapable of honest work, and he received neither compensation nor sick pay. But if you are well enough to go shoplifting and car-breaking, you are well enough to go to normal work, or at least to seek normal work. A shoplifter is not a victim just because he finds it easier to shoplift than to find and do work.

Shoplifting is not very high up on the scale of human evil, of course, but training children up to such a life is far from anodyne. The fact that Shota turns against it because he comes to realise that it is wrong suggest that an awareness of the necessity of the *meum* and *tuum* is almost inborn in humans and can be overridden only with effort — an effort that should not be made.

Moreover, one of the members of the jolly band, Nobuyo, is actually a murderess, albeit of an abusive man. It is possible that her killing was in some way justifiable or at least extenuated, but only if killing him were the sole way of escaping his abuse. We are not sufficiently informed to know whether or not this was so in this case, but the presumption must surely be against it. If his abuse were her defence in a trial, one would not simply accept her word but demand evidence of it.

As to the supposed subversiveness of the film with regard to bourgeois or nuclear family, it (the film) is surely more subtle than that. True, in every example of such a family present in the film there is betrayal, abandonment or violence, but in the end the same is true of the reconstituted family as well. In other words, these unpleasant realities are possible in all forms of human association, none of which will therefore ever be perfect.

The two children in the story are genuine victims, the first of abandonment, the second of flagrant maltreatment. But are these things more, or less, frequent in normal, bourgeois families than in other possibly types of intimate association? Surely less. To demand perfection of human institutions such that no abuse occurs within them is to demand that there should be no institutions. It is only when abuses are widespread and easily to be eliminated that they cast doubt on the legitimacy of the institutions in which they occur, and the point at which this is reached is always a matter of judgment.

In other words, this film is not highly subversive, except of my own preconceptions. It subverted, for instance, my supposition that in small matters such as table manners, even the poor in Japan are refined. But in the film, they are shown eating with a singular lack of such refinement, to put it very mildly. Perhaps the critics would rejoice at lumpenproletariat warmth of heart, but they would not bring up their own children to follow suit. Thus, the film is not so much subversive as the occasion for reflection, a much higher aim. Not all reflection is subversive, and not all subversion is reflective.

27

LES HÉRITIÈRES, DIR. MARCELO MARTINESSI, PARAGUAY

It is rarely that one has the opportunity to see a Paraguayan film, and I seized it with alacrity.

If people did but know it, Paraguay has one of the most astounding histories of any country in the world. Its first leader as an independent state, Dr José Gaspar Rodriguez de Francia, known as *El Supremo*, ruled for twenty-six years and has a claim to be the first modern totalitarian dictator. He was the first such dictator to find foreign intellectual apologists, most notably Thomas Carlyle, who wrote an essay about him whose argument was the rough equivalent of those who admired Mussolini because he made the trains run on time. Even now in Paraguay he has his defenders, usually nationalists of a socialist bent: they praise his policy of autarkic economic development, so different from anything the country experienced afterwards. For them, the end justified the tyranny: the closing of the borders, the forced interracial marriages, the universal spying.

El Supremo was followed by the fat Carlos Antonio López, who ruled for a further twenty years and was said by the American ambassador to be so fond of his country that he owned half of it, again proving that Paraguay was in advance of its time. His son, Francisco Solano López, took over from his father and led his country into one of the most disastrous wars in human history, the War of the Triple Alliance. In this war of Paraguay against Brazil, Argentina and Uruguay over nothing very much, provoked unnecessarily by López, Paraguay lost at least nine-tenths of its male population, being thereafter known as the Land of Women. 'I die with my country!' were López's last words, and there is still an equestrian statue of him in heroic pose in Asunción, the capital, uttering these immortal words — or at least there was the last time I was in Asunción many years ago.

This film makes no reference to any of the above or subsequent history, most of it also disastrous, though oddly enough hardly any men appear in it, and those few only with walk-on parts. It was as if parthenogenesis were already the norm. Perhaps Paraguay is once more the Land of Women.

The plot of the film is simple. Two aging lesbians, Chela and Chiquita, live in a spacious but decaying house in Asunción. They inherited money but through inattention or mismanagement, presumably, they have fallen on hard times and have to sell most of their precious possessions. In addition, Chiquita is accused of fraud by her bank. The nature of this alleged fraud is not clear but is probably that of obtaining a loan on false information, not necessarily provided with dishonest intent. She is condemned to a period in prison.

Chela is left on her own in the melancholy house. She paints a little, but not with enough seriousness or talent to make a living from it. One day, while Chiquita is still imprisoned, a rich neighbour asks Chela whether she would be so good as to drive her to her bridge party. Chela agrees, though she has not driven her old Mercedes for a long time and no longer has a driving licence. The rich neighbour gives Chela some money, saying to save appearances that it is for the fuel, but really as payment. Presumably the neighbour is aware that Chela has fallen on hard times and does not want to humiliate her. Before long, Chela is running an informal taxi service for a group of rich ladies.

On one of her regular excursions, Chela meets a younger woman called Angy. The latter has boyfriends, but none of them satisfactory (of course). Chela becomes emotionally attached to Angy, whom she meets regularly at the whist games to which she has driven her rich ladies and then as a customer for her taxi service. She falls in love with Angy, though how far Angy reciprocates is left ambiguous.

Then Chiquita is released from prison and returns home. Chela is not as pleased to see her or as welcoming as she ought to be. On the contrary, Chiquita, who snores when asleep, almost disgusts her. One fine morning, Chiquita finds Chela gone, and the car with her. This is the end of the film, and we are left to decide for ourselves whether Chela finds happiness or even freedom by leaving, or even whether she has left for good or will return.

The best scenes in the film are undoubtedly those in the women's prison in which Chiquita is for a time imprisoned. There is certainly more life in the prison than in the circle of rich ladies for which Chela drives. There is noise, madness, laughter, vitality, song and violence in the prison;[27] the bourgeois ladies, by comparison, seem staid and lifeless, as if bridge were the means by which they fill their time not too unpleasantly until they die, a female version of golf. Chiquita has little difficulty in adapting to life in prison, less difficulty in fact than Chela has in visiting it.

I have visited South American prisons, and they are as depicted in the film. On the one hand they are frightening, inasmuch as violence can break out at any time (I was told in Lurigancho Prison in Lima that it cost $10 to have someone killed there, not an immense sum even then); on the other hand, there is also a sense of freedom in them, in the sense than no one seeks to regulate or impose discipline on the prisoners, as they try to do in western prisons. If you don't mind the noise, the promiscuous association with hundreds of others (to an extent avoidable if you have the money), and if you are quick to grasp the underlying informal rules, then life in what seem to be terrible institutions becomes in many ways preferable or more bearable than in our more rigid penitentiaries, at least for people who value their freedom (which not all do). The worst is far, far worse, but the average or median may be better.

What does this film 'mean', assuming that it does not intend to tell a story at random? At no point is it very cheerful, let

---

[27] My little experience of women's prisons suggests that they are worse than men's. Perhaps this is because only the very worst of women are sent to them, whereas this is not so of men. In men's prisons, the worst are diluted by the not so bad.

alone funny, and can hardly have been intended merely to amuse. In an interview, the director recalled that the bourgeoisie in Paraguay was complicit with dictatorships (when I was there for the first time Alfredo Stroessner was still president, seemingly for eternity, and I arrived in Puerto Stroessner on the M.V. Alfredo Stroessner to the strains of the Alfredo Stroessner Polka).[28] But even if this were true in some abstract sense, in that many of that class preferred the dictatorship they had to what they believed was the likely alternative, I did not see any real symbolism of this in the film, any connection of political dictatorship with the events portrayed, which seemed largely of a private nature. If Chiquita was wrongly accused of fraud (and this is by no means certain), the injustice was intra-bourgeois, as it were, rather than a case of the bourgeoisie oppressing the poor. Nor is there any hint in the film of political terror: there is only daily life interrupted by the system of criminal justice, as it might be anywhere. And insofar as the prison is terrifying, it is because of the inmates, not because of warders, the agents of the state. In fact, it is terrifying because of an *absence* of agents of the state, an interesting fact for political philosophers.

In fact, the story is a rather banal one, at least for someone who has worked in a penitentiary. Quite often I would be

---

[28] This recalls to mind the wonderful ironic title of Ernesto Cardenal's poem, *Somoza desveliza la estatua de Somoza en el estadio Somoza* (Somoza unveils the statue of Somoza in the Somoza Stadium.)

asked to see a prisoner who had suddenly become suicidal because he had received what was known as a *Dear John*. This was a letter informing him that his girlfriend, though she still loved him *to bits*, had moved in with the man next door or down the road, and that they — the former girlfriend and the prisoner — were no longer *together*, to use the term of art. Grief quite often turned swiftly to anger, and the girlfriend was accused of what she had always been, a promiscuous slag or slut. Nor is it altogether surprising that a prison term often breaks a couple apart, for it is a rude interruption of the routine that often keeps the couple together. Inertia, if I may be allowed a contradiction, is a powerful force in human affairs.

What is intended to lift the story above the level of banality, of course, is that Chiquita and Chela are lesbians. Since they have lived together for thirty years, which would take them back to the late-Stroessner period, apparently without having experienced any great difficulties, it might be concluded that Paraguayan society was in this respect rather tolerant, especially as, being so small a country population-wise, the real relations of the couple could hardly have escaped notice, all the more so as they had at least one live-in servant who was unlikely to have kept everything to herself and never to have gossiped. But I doubt (though I may be wrong) that the tolerance of Paraguayan society was the message that the director wanted to convey.

On the contrary, the film was made, at least partially, with funds proved by the European Union, as was the film previously discussed, *Retablo*.[29]

It seemed odd to me that films with strongly homosexual themes or content should have emerged at the same time. If I were given to conspiracy theories, I might suggest that this was more than mere coincidence, that there was some concerted plan, or at least evangelistic intent, behind it. I am insufficiently *au fait* with the current situation in Peru and Paraguay, whether the intelligentsia is preoccupied with the position of homosexuality in their respective countries, or whether (as seems more likely to me) directors and screen-writers, in need of funds, realise that such themes are more likely to receive such funds. If my surmise is correct, which I freely admit that it might not be, the films in a sense tell us as much or more about Europe than about the countries in which they take place.

It seems that we might here be in the presence of an ideology, or at least the simulacrum or pale imitation of an ideology. It is a commonplace that European societies, especially at their summits, have lost their religious bearings, indeed rejected them altogether, and are in search of a transcendent common meaning, purpose and ethical

------

[29] So was another film that I have not included, *Rafiki*, a film about lesbian love in Kenya and the outraged violence that it provokes, and that was banned in that country because it was said to 'promote' lesbianism. The ban was lifted for seven days so that the film might be entered for a film festival whose rules stated that all entries had had to be shown to the public for at least seven days. During those seven days it drew large crowds in Nairobi, probably because it had been banned.

framework. Their best stab at it (not a very good one) is a doctrine of human rights and the search for victims whose rights have been infringed. No sooner discovered, these rights become both backdatedly universal and immemorial, and countries and societies that do not respect them (because they haven't caught up with the latest fashion in moral enthusiasm) are subject to propaganda bought with public funds.

Whether the European taxpayer would want his forced contributions to be used in this fashion is another question to which I do not know the answer. But then, of course, the answer hardly matters. The European taxpayer should shut his mouth and let his moral superiors, the distributor of funds to far-flung places, get on with it.

28

DONBASS, DIR. SERGEI LOZNITSA, UKRAINE

War is chaotic, and it is only after it is over, if then, that most people who live through it discern its pattern. This is so *a fortiori* in civil war in which there are so many currents and counter-currents and in which there is often foreign interference as well as internal conflict. The literature of the Spanish Civil War is immense, and practically nothing of its historiography is settled beyond dispute eighty years after its end. Perhaps it never will be: certainly books about it continue to pour from the press in an unceasing torrent beyond the capacity of any one person to absorb, giving rise to new controversies.

The current war in the Ukraine is complex and divides opinion very strongly. Everyone wants to see a good side and a bad, Man being a natural Manichaean. A slightly better and a worse is not sufficient to meet our desires, which are for moral clarity.

This film was directed by a Ukrainian (again with European funds so that it was unlikely that he would depart very obviously or too openly from the official view of the European Union). Nevertheless, it cannot be viewed, at least in my opinion, as a simple condemnation of the Russian separatists and their Russian backers, though it is certainly not flattering to them either. From the aspect of humanity and generosity of spirit, there is not much more to be expected of the Ukrainians than of the Russians. To believe, as some critics apparently did, that the film is mere propaganda for the Ukrainian state is like reading the poems of Wilfred Owen as anti-German.

The action of the film takes place in or very near the separatist enclave in eastern Ukraine, a self-proclaimed republic, where the majority of the population is Russian. The film is episodic in nature: there is no thread of a single narrative that runs through it. We see, for example, a session of a municipal council that ends in chaos, an underground bomb shelter in which a large number of civilians take refuge, a marriage that is celebrated in a small town of the self-proclaimed republic, a scene in a maternity hospital laying bare administrative corruption, the torture by passers-by of a captured Ukrainian soldier tied to a lamppost in a Russian town, and the abuse of a German journalist who is trying to enter the Russian war zone to report on the war.

The episodic nature of the film might be — probably is — an attempt to capture the incomprehensibility, or difficulty in grasping the totality, of the war by any single person or by those caught up in it. This seems to me reasonable, a good device, while at the same time not forgetting that the function of the intellect is to order raw phenomena into some kind of pattern. And the episodes do encourage us to think of an underlying meaning. The pattern is the pity of war.

Let us take the episode of the German journalist first. He is trying to enter the separatist republic, and it is quite clear from his manner that he expects, as a journalist, to be treated as a different order of being from the normal foreign traveller (if any such there be in this situation). He is, at least in his own estimation, doing God's work, or whatever his equivalent of God might be. His *bona fides* cannot be doubted simply by virtue of his profession. But by coincidence, I saw the film in the week in which a German journalist, Claas Relotius, who wrote for the most important and prestigious German news magazine, *Der Spiegel*, and who won at least four prizes for his reportage, was exposed as a fraud, having written at least fourteen stories for the magazine that were complete fabrications.

When in the film the journalist and his interpreter arrive at the checkpoint of the separatist state, the Russian soldiers manning it have a completely different conception of the war correspondent from his own, thinking of him more as a voyeur or careerist or even spy than as truth-teller to the world. War for the soldiers is more than a matter of mere observation, and my opinion of the war correspondent's metier is closer to that of the soldiers than to that of the correspondent himself. If there are wars, there must be (I suppose, at least ever since the Crimean War, when William Howard Russell invented the genre of war reportage) war correspondents. But having myself reported from two or three war zones, I can attest that it puts all other kind of work into the shade from the point of view of excitement, and it is all too easy to persuade oneself that by informing the waiting world, as one imagines oneself to be doing, one is doing the world's work. More often than not, however, the world does not reciprocate this sense of importance, or self-importance.

But in the film, the war correspondent suffers another disadvantage: he is German. A bearded Russian, who might from his appearance have been a soldier of the Tsar, harangues him. Being German, he is, *ex officio*, a fascist, or at least if not a fascist himself, his grandfather must have been one. And of course the fascists — or more properly, the Nazis — were defeated by men such as the bearded Russian.

For the man who is haranguing, the present war is likewise a war against fascism, as if the Second World War had never ended. For him, the Ukrainian state is fascist — as, I suspect, he thinks everywhere except Russia is. The Germans support Ukraine in the war, at least verbally, therefore no further proof is needed. Guilt by association is the highest form of proof.

There is, of course, a history behind his attitude, to put it mildly. It is true that many Ukrainians welcomed the Nazi invasion and served it; they were scarcely less antisemitic than the Nazis themselves. But at the same time, they had no reason to be grateful to the Russians, or rather the Soviets, who organised a peace-time famine for them of gigantic proportions. The intellectuals in the West were perfectly well-informed of this famine[30] but chose to disregard it because it interfered with their world-view. For an intellectual, a world-view is worth more than the world.

Thus, in this conflict, the Ukrainians think of the Russians

---

[30] In my collection of books about the Soviet Union in the 1920s and 30s, I have books complete with photographs of massacres and the dead from famine, the latter piled up much as the dead were in Buchenwald.

as unreconstructed Bolsheviks who intend to starve the Ukrainians once more, while the Russians think the Ukrainians are fascists thirsting for revenge who will take the first opportunity to cleanse the Ukraine ethnically. Each side plays victim of the other, without recognition of the wrongs perpetrated by its own side. And, as La Rochefoucauld says, we never forgive those whom we have wronged. It is all too easy, pleasurable in fact, to suppose that the descendants of people who have done evil must themselves be evil, not only the sins of the fathers being handed down, but the causes of the sins of the fathers being handed down, to the nth generation.

In the midst of all the horror there is an unexpected comic or satirical scene, that of the wedding in the breakaway republic. The bride is a porcine, crudely made-up, vulgar, obese woman carrying a bouquet of artificial flowers, the groom a slight, ineffectual, rather stupid man, both of them in what would have passed in Soviet days as ceremonial finery, that is to say cheap and nastily-produced kitsch.

The bride arrives for the civil ceremony at the neoclassical town hall in one of those vulgar white stretch limousines which are considered by the proletarians of the world (they are united at least in this) to be the acme of elegant luxury. Gunfire into the air greets her arrival, another symptom of malignant bad taste. The woman who conducts the ceremony, also dressed in vulgar finery but much less vulgar in manner, tries to keep control of it but is constantly interrupted by the crude hilarity of the bride. At the end of the ceremony, the whole congregation breaks out into the separatists' 'national' anthem, not quite spontaneously as the instrumental accompaniment is recorded and relayed though the public address system in the hall.

The whole episode might be regarded as an unsubtle satire on the Russians of the Donetsk region: some critics called it surreal. I cannot say what were the director's intentions, not being party to his mind, but for me the scene was rather a depiction of the enduring aesthetic — or rather, anti-aesthetic — effects of Soviet rule, probably as enduring in the Ukraine proper, under Ukrainian rule, as in the Donetsk region. And if there is exaggeration in the scene, it is not by much.

Perhaps the most startling and dramatic episode of the whole film is that in which a Ukrainian prisoner, draped around his shoulders in a tattered Ukrainian flag, is tied by two Russian soldiers to a lamppost in the middle of a provincial town. He has a notice draped around his neck also to the effect that he was a 'punisher', whatever that might imply, presumably an interrogator of Russian captives.

Having tied him to the lamppost, the accompanying soldiers await developments, knowing, of course, what they are likely to be. A group of young thugs — looking at them, one can't help thinking that there was something to Lombroso's theories after all — drive up in a car, get out and at first abuse and humiliate the captive by blowing cigarette smoke in his face and then by taking selfies with him as they pull him about. The mere fact that these young men believe that creating a permanent record of themselves being cruel to a helpless prisoner will never rebound on them, and indeed is something that they might one day show proudly to their children or grandchildren, is indicative of the cultural, moral and intellectual level to which they have descended. One shudders for mankind.

A crowd gathers round the prisoner. An old lady with a stick pokes her way through it and repeatedly plunges her stick into the prisoner's abdomen and chest. She is applauded for this as if she had done something brave and heroic, and certainly, it is not what one expects of old ladies. Then a middle-aged lady comes forward — she says that she has lost children in the war, and there is no suggestion that she is lying — and demands a confession from the soldier. It is not forthcoming: by now he has been so badly beaten that he could hardly have uttered it if he had wanted to. The crowd loses all its remaining self-control, never very strong. It calls for him to be hanged, and young men smash their fists into his face and stomach with the maximum of their force. You feel that they are going to kill him, but the two soldiers in whose custody he is untie him and lead him away. They have brought him to be punished but not executed. Are they merely obeying orders, or is there some faint remnant of human decency in them? We do not discover.

The Russian separatists are portrayed very unsympathetically, but I at any rate had little confidence that their enemies were very much better — or, indeed, that the film intended us to think so. After all, the Russians and Ukrainians are very close linguistically and culturally, for decades sharing a history of totalitarian oppression and misery. They are physically indistinguishable, and everything about them (from uniforms to systems of bribery) are all but identical. Would a Russian captive have been better treated by the Ukrainians?

We see a group of Ukrainian refugee civilians living in a dilapidated, underground bomb shelter. During one of the

Chechen wars, I saw Chechen refugees living in similar, though not quite as bad, conditions. The Ukrainian refugees live on bunk beds in crowded, damp and dark tunnels, in which every cough and sneeze spreads disease. They have little to do but wait.

Into these wretched conditions intrudes a young woman whose dress and manner are typical of that of a Soviet-era prostitute such as used to hang out in the lobby of the Intourist Hotel (now demolished) in Moscow, hoping to ensnare a westerner. By providing her services to separatists, the young woman has access to rare groceries. She comes to extract her mother from the shelter, telling her that she (the daughter) will keep her in comfortable surroundings. To the daughter's fury, her mother will not leave: she will not profit from either treachery or prostitution. The daughter is unattractive, but one cannot altogether condemn her. Who can say how he would behave in the *sauve-qui-peut* of war?

If the film had been intended as mere propaganda, it fails (thank goodness). This is because a mirror-image film could all too easily be imagined. My film, the director could with justice have said, is the drama of war and the pity of war. The drama is in the pity.

29

LE POIRIER SAUVAGE, DIR. NURI BILGE CEYLAN, TURKEY

Attacks on materialism are so frequent (materialism not in the philosophical sense, that reality is entirely material, but in the sense that money, possessions and physical comforts are the proper or only end of life) that it is almost refreshing to be reminded that all that is not materialistic is not therefore admirable or worthwhile.

Sinan, the protagonist of this film, is a young man who returns home to a town in western Turkey after he has completed his studies to be a teacher like his father. But he despises the town, despises his father, and considers himself much above both because he wants to be a writer. In fact, he has written a book and is in search of funds to have it published.

Sinan is not an attractive character. The film is three hours long, but during it he hardly smiles, let alone laughs. It is true that his prospects are not altogether rosy, but we do not see him chatting amiably with friends, joking with his sister, or anything similar. He lacks charm and (we suspect) the talent that might make a writer of him. He likes to read but gives no evidence of any particular intellectual capacity or even interests. For him, his desire to be a writer is, perhaps, more urgent than anything that he has to say. This, by the way, is a far from uncommon pattern. I used to have young patients who told me that they wanted to be writers or artists but who, when I asked them what they read or which galleries they visited, said that they wanted to be writers or artists, not readers or art critics. They had the idea that, deep within them, was a source of genius and originality that would manifest itself sooner or later, generally sooner, that would be inhibited by mere knowledge.

Sinan's father is not altogether admirable, either. An inveterate gambler, he is constantly in debt to the point that the electricity bill goes unpaid and the electricity gets cut off. People in the town dun Sinan for the money his father owes them, which not surprisingly he finds humiliating. (In one scene, Sinan's father sits in a café in the town which relays horse-racing on its flat-screen television. I did not know that they had western-style horse-racing in Turkey, which illustrates my depth of knowledge about it despite having visited it about fifteen times. Islam frowns upon gambling, and given the temper of the times in Turkey, one wonders how long the sport of kings — or fools — can survive there.)

Sinan remonstrates with his father and even insults him, without recognising his good qualities of which his mother reminds him: his father is kind, has never so much as raised a hand to him, does not drink, and so forth. He is weak rather than bad. But there is another accusation against him that his son levies against him: now retired, he is engaged on a futile search for water on the land owned by *his* father, Sinan's grandfather, just outside the town, water that would make the land valuable.

Sinan's father has been told by the local peasants that there is no water to be had from the subsoil, but still he obstinately persists in digging for it. He dreams that the land will become fertile, the crops profitable and his debts paid. But it is a forlorn hope, much like that of the gambler who stakes his last few coins or chips on a single throw in the hope that it will restore his fortunes.

Sinan takes his manuscript, titled *Le Poirier Sauvage (The Wild Peartree)*, round to anyone who might conceivably finance its publication. First, he tries the mayor, who receives him not unkindly, but says that, since the book is not intended to promote tourism to the town or district, he cannot use the town's money on such a venture, though the sum requested is very little. But he suggests that the author apply to the local businessman made good, who is supposedly an avid reader.

The ensuing interview is a painful one. The businessman is uneducated and self-made, something of a Josiah Bounderby of Coketown in manner. He left school earlier than his fellows, and those who continued their studies did far less well in life than he (as measured, of course, by their income and what they possess). Some of those who studied now work for him, and two have even committed suicide. Education is not necessarily the road to success.

We have already learned the truth of the businessman's homily to Sinan because, though he has graduated, Sinan has to take another exam to become a teacher, there being 300,000 more graduates as teachers than posts to place them in. Though the prize, a teaching post wherever in the country the state designates it, is by no means glittering, those who do not succeed in the exam must do their military service, often in the war-torn east, a prospect not viewed with much enthusiasm by young Turkish men such as Sinan.

The businessman listens to Sinan with sympathy at first. Sinan says that he has heard that he is a keen reader, and the businessman points to some shelves in his office on which are ranged a few books of the kind that no one who could be called a keen reader would have. The businessman says that, with the economic situation being so difficult these days, he has no time now to read (in reality, of course, he has never read), and the gulf between his and Sinan's view of the world becomes all too clear. His view is prosaic, crudely utilitarian and purely economistic: what does not lead to more money is not worth doing. But whether his decision not to help Sinan is good or bad depends on the quality of what Sinan has written, which we suspect is not high. It is not the non-materialistic end of an endeavour that gives it value.

Sinan goes to the town's bookshop, which is rather an impressive establishment (far better than you would find in an English town of such a size). On its walls are large posters of Gabriel García Marquez, Virginia Woolf and Franz Kafka, which suggests that there are more people in the town with literary interests than Sinan, with his adolescent sense of superiority, is prepared to admit. Working on the balcony of the shop is the most famous local writer, apparently a great success, and obviously a man of high intelligence — higher that Sinan's.

Sinan buttonholes him and will not let him escape. Sinan is completely oblivious to the writer's obvious desire to bring their conversation to a close so that he can get on with his work, and to his growing irritation. Sinan asks him whether he would read his manuscript. When the writer replies that he cannot possibly read all the manuscripts submitted to him because, if he did so, he would have no time to write his own books, Sinan, now irritated himself, says that wouldn't necessarily be a pity, trying then to recover from this gaffe by saying that it was only a joke.

This is hardly the way to the writer's heart, however, and Sinan is so self-absorbed that when the writer, forced by his importuning, packs up his things and leaves the shop, Sinan, still impervious to social signals, follows him and tortures him with further questions and reflections. By the end of their encounter, one would have understood it if the writer had hit Sinan.

The scene is very painful for anyone who has ever been an adolescent.

Sinan's father is devoted to his dog, a fine animal, but Sinan, still obsessed by his need to publish his book, steals the dog and sells it, using the proceeds to have five hundred copies printed. He places some in the local bookshop, but not a single one sells. The distress he has caused his father by the loss of his beloved dog has been for nothing. (Sinan discussed the question of how far an author may hurt those around him in the name of literature with the writer in the bookshop.)

The time for Sinan's military service arrives. We see only a very brief snapshot of him in military green patrolling the bleak and snow-swept hills of eastern Turkey. There is no reference to the justice or otherwise of Turkey's military activity, or of the Kurdish (or the Kurdish leadership's) struggle against the Turkish state.

Sinan returns home once more, this time from the army rather than from college, now somewhat smartened up. His father has received a lump sum as part of his pension, which has allowed him to pay off his debts. He and his wife now live separately, she in the house in town, he on his father's piece of land, in a primitive and ramshackle house.

To his surprise, Sinan discovers that his father has in the meantime read his book and is even able to quote from it. His father asks him why he should be surprised, to which Sinan replies that he, his father, is the first person he has met who ever read it. This remark is the first indication that Sinan is able to take some distance from himself and to view the world with detachment and even a little irony. His father, too, has changed: he has accepted that it is pointless to continue to dig wells in the land in the hope of getting rich quick. He is now content to work the land as everyone else around him does. No more dreams of sudden success.

The end of the film is enigmatic. In the penultimate scene, we briefly see Sinan having hanged himself in a useless well. This comes as a surprise because he has been reconciled with his father. Perhaps he realises how badly he treated, and how harshly he judged, him. Perhaps the defeat of his literary ambition has forced him to face up to the fact that he is an ordinary person, in no way superior to his surroundings. Despair and guilt drive him to put an end to his days.

But in the very last scene, we see Sinan alive again, this time working with a pickaxe at the bottom of his father's dry well. He is digging for water — whether from conviction that his father was right all along, or as an act of remorse, we do not know.

The film is a cinematographic *Bildungsroman*, the story of two men's painful education in how to live, their place in the world, and what is worth doing or achieving. How many young men must have experienced something analogous to Sinan's trajectory? How many must have been forced by the harsh reality of the world to abandon their exaggerated conception of themselves? I hesitate to say that the film deals with a universal theme: the problem of adolescence arises only in modern societies in which people have to find a place and believe that they can find it where they want, rather than having a place ascribed to them from birth, as in primitive or caste societies. Both types of societies have their problems, there being no perfect or permanent satisfaction for Mankind. Sinan's problem at the end of the film, perhaps, is that he is becoming resigned to a life without contentment. There is nothing wrong with being fatalistic, so long as one accepts one's fate, but fatalism without acceptance is (if I may so put it) a wretched fate.

As we left the cinema, my wife and I, we both thought of a lesson or moral that the film might be said to have taught, and that the maker probably did not intend: namely, that military service is good for young men such as Sinan. Certainly he is a much better (and more attractive) figure after he has completed it than he was before, and it is impossible not to believe that it was his military service that improved him. This would be an uncongenial message to many, and I pass it on without being in the least militaristic: I am far too egotistic myself not to have hated military life. Indeed, I think I should have spent most of my time in military prison, for I have never been able to abide orders that seemed to me stupid.[31]

How did military service do Sinan good? The answer is simple. For the first time in his life, he had to stop thinking about himself to the exclusion of practically everything else. Patrolling those hills in the fear of ambush put his mental travails into some kind of perspective. Whereas before he was constantly trying to find himself (on the assumption that there was something wonderful to find), now he lost himself and, paradoxically, routine, discipline, fear and danger lifted a great weight from his shoulders. Do not seek to find yourself, seek to lose yourself.

---

[31] The beneficial effects of national service in France are laid out in a best-selling book, *L'Archipel français*, by Jérôme Fourquet.

30

DIAMANTINO, DIRS. GABRIEL ABRANTES AND DANIEL SCHMIDT, PORTUGAL

This film begins with a lie: namely, that none of the characters in it is intended to resemble any living person, when it is perfectly obvious, even to me who knows little of modern football, that the Diamantino of the title is closely modelled on Cristiano Ronaldo, the Portuguese player who is currently one of the most famous — and most highly-paid — players in the world. The actor who plays Diamantino is so similar physically to Ronaldo that one could easily believe him to be his brother, almost even his twin. Like Ronaldo, Diamantino has diamond studs in his ears: evidently, he is not called Diamantino for nothing.

Falsus in uno, falsus in omnibus? (This is the old legal principle, now no longer accepted in most jurisdictions, that if a witness lies in one thing, the rest of his testimony about anything whatever is not to be believed.) The false disclaimer at the very outset of the film makes one wonder whether the next disclaimer, that in the making of the film none of the animals that appeared in it, principally Pekinese dogs, had been abused, is similarly false, and that in fact they were severely abused.

Practically everything about this film is false. It straddles several genres without settling on any, and while one cannot demand that a work of art or the imagination should be pigeonholed in a fixed genre, the different genres in a single work should at least meld into a coherent artistic whole, which *Diamantino* certainly does not. It is difficult, for example, to say when its mockery of kitsch becomes kitsch itself.

The plot of the film is difficult to relate. Diamantino is a gifted footballer as naïve as Candide but now extremely rich. He has made an enormous fortune which is managed by his wicked identical twin sisters. The day before he is to appear in the final of the World Cup for Portugal against Sweden, he is on his yacht. He has an epiphany when he sees a little boat full of asylum-seekers (so-called, though they are probably economic migrants), more than an average number of which is female. Male migrants are usually more numerous, but females tug more at the heartstrings.

Diamantino, who has a good heart maintained and nourished by ignorance, naivety and a natural sentimentality, not only rescues them but, being loveless and apparently sexless, dreams of adopting a little black boy as a son, much as a child wants to attach himself to a soft toy on to which he can project love that is reciprocated, without any of the inconvenient tensions that attend love of a real human being.

Diamantino is suspected by the authorities of tax evasion (as was Ronaldo, who was eventually forced to pay the Spanish tax-gatherers some sixteen million Euros, a mere drop in his ocean of money). Two female secret police agents, one white, one black (lesbian lovers, of course), are investigating his possible tax fraud. Knowing of his desire to adopt a little black boy as a son, the black policewoman, who happens to be a specialist in informatics, poses as a young male refugee, and her lesbian lover as a nun who runs an orphanage for refugees. Diamantino takes the police-agent-cum-refugee into his home, a beautiful and isolated Portuguese baroque palace, footballers such as he being the new aristocracy, though his tastes in food and decoration are still strictly proletarian.

But Diamantino in the meantime has gone from being a national hero to being deeply reviled because, being so troubled by his epiphany, he misses a penalty kick in the final that would have brought Portugal's score level with Sweden's and thereby saved the match. Just as Diamantino strides up to take the penalty kick, he is distracted by a vision of a giant, long-haired Pekinese dog guarding the goal, and fluffs the kick. National despair when he does so could not be more complete: it is worse than defeat in war.

Diamantino is not only naïve, he is not very bright. (I doubt that Ronaldo would be very pleased by being depicted as childishly pea-brained, but perhaps he is past caring.) The police agent insinuated into his house, with whom Diamantino's relations amount almost to would-be pederasty, discovers that it is not he but his wicked sisters who evade taxes by a complex system of international transfers of money.

Meanwhile they, the wicked sisters, are trying to make use of Diamantino in propaganda for a far-right movement that is campaigning for Portugal's exit from the European Union. They also take him to a high-tech, genetic engineering laboratory (a glass building not entirely like I. M. Pei's pyramid in the Louvre), where he is to be cloned so that an unbeatable Portuguese team of eleven Diamantinos, also to be used for nationalistic purposes, can be trained. In the course of his investigations and treatment that he undergoes in the laboratory, he starts to develop women's breasts, or at least to suffer from gynaecomastia. In several scenes, he is almost crucified by the chief scientist, a woman called Dr Lamborghini, the same name as the manufacturer of his canary-yellow sports car of pharaonic cost.

There is some kind of race between the black police agent and the wicked sisters to rescue Diamantino, but there is not too much tension as to the outcome, nor do we much care, since there is no reality to the story. In the last scene, Diamantino cavorts naked on a beach with the police agent, both of them in love, though because of or despite his gynaecomastia is not made clear.

This is all a terrible artistic mish-mash, funded largely by the Portuguese state. By the end of the film one feels as if one's mind has been put through the psychological equivalent of a food mixer. But just as a *velouté* has a taste, so this mish-mash has a connotation, that of some kind of political correctness.

For example, there is the question of whether the physical rescue of the migrants is really necessary. After all, they have got all the way from Africa to within a few hundred yards of the Portuguese coast at a point where it is not dangerous. Feelings of compassion towards them as individuals are decent and virtuous, but this reaction is surely not enough when we consider the matter of such migration more widely and deeply.

How did the people in the dinghy arrive at the coast? Who or what were they fleeing, or were they merely attracted by the prospect of a standard of living much higher than their own? (This attraction is not dishonourable in itself, of course.) How much did they pay for their passage, and to whom? It would almost certainly have been a sum that put them in the upper economic quintile of their fellow citizens. How many such people should Europe welcome every year? A thousand, a million, ten million? This latter is a very unpleasant question, because no one undertakes so hazardous a journey without good reason. And yet it must be asked. Simply avoiding it because it is unpleasant is not a solution, far from it. Mere good-heartedness is not enough.

Diamantino wants a child to love and a child who will love him in return. There is nothing intrinsically wrong with this desire, of course, but it is surely possible to wonder whether Diamantino's method of fulfilling it is legitimate. It reminds me of the young patients I used to see, hardly more than girls, who had had children at a very early age — fifteen, say — because they had emerged from so loveless a world that the only way they could think of achieving reciprocated love was to have a baby irrespective of who the father was (it being more or less taken for granted that he would clear off soon afterwards, almost always a justified assumption). Diamantino's immense wealth would protect his adopted child from the consequences of fulfilling the desire for a child in this fashion, but there is a taboo against saying that what is permissible to the rich is impermissible to the poor. In any case one may wonder whether Diamantino's love for such a child would endure into its adolescence.

Diamantino, thanks to his good heart and his desire for love, takes in (what he supposes to be) a young refugee: good. But what happens to the others whom he does not take in?

They, of course, will probably be kept at public expense, that is to say from the forced contributions of people with modest incomes. If such migrants arrive in large numbers, there will be overcrowding. We see Diamantino's supposed refugee 'child' in a spacious baroque palace, but it is a fair bet that Diamantino would not want his palace overrun with such refugees, for what then would be the point of owning it?

The far-right movement in the film (let us not forget that fascism is as much of the left as of the right) advocates the exit of Portugal from the European Union, thus implying that only xenophobes and fascists could possibly be opposed to 'ever closer union' of twenty-seven countries under the direction of perpetual and irremovable elite. No doubt there are things to be said in favour of the European Union, but surely there are things to be said against it too by people other than brown- or blackshirts.

It is hardly news that professional footballers are not, on the whole, very gifted intellectually. One no more expects them to be highly intelligent than one expects mathematicians to be champion weightlifters (though some may be). But I did learn at least one thing from this film that perhaps I should not have needed to be taught. The actor who plays Diamantino in the film has a physique very similar to that of Ronaldo. In the matter of fitness and physical strength, he seems almost identical, and far, far above average. And yet, when he is filmed in short sequences as if he were playing football, one sees at once the great gulf fixed between him and Ronaldo. He has not the grace of Ronaldo, his movements are contrived rather than flowing, he is playing at playing football, rather than playing football. Ronaldo's gift is not just in strength and fitness and willingness to train, though all these are necessary; it is a natural aptitude, an aptitude that comes from we know not where, but that we should once have called God-given. This aptitude is not the highest kind of human genius (though it is very nearly the highest-paid), but it is a kind of genius nonetheless — something that, before watching this film, I had not quite fully appreciated.

31

PEU M'IMPORTE SI L'HISTOIRE NOUS CONSIDÈRE COMME DES BARBARES, DIR. RADU JUDE, ROMANIA

Having visited Romania shortly before the downfall of Ceausescu, I developed an interest in the country, particularly in its pre-war intellectual history. Many European countries had their fascistic writers, but in few were they as prominent, even predominant, as in Romania. Writers who later emigrated and became world-famous, such as Emil Cioran[32] and Mircea Eliade, had their strongly fascist phase and wrote things that made Donald Trump seem namby-pamby by comparison, and that are so hateful — full of hate — that on

---

[32] You could interpret Cioran's subsequent career as a writer in French, his third language after Romanian and German but which he so mastered that he is considered one of the finest prose stylists in French of the Twentieth Century, as having been a long process of atonement for, or less charitably, cover-up of, some of the nastiest pages ever written by a cultivated man. He wrote – in French – as someone existentially disabused, as it were, but was he disabused not so much with life and the world, from which he felt, or feigned, a weary detachment, as with himself? It is one thing to be wrong, as we all sometimes are, and another to have been wrong in such a way as he.

reading them one begins to sympathise a little with the form of censorship known as political correctness. Some things should not be said, and Romanian intellectuals said them.

How far the expression of abominable ideas leads to abominable actions is a moot point, of course; but that the Romanian state, and therefore Romanians, committed abominable atrocities during the war cannot be disputed. Their alliance with Nazi Germany allowed them to occupy Bessarabia and Transnistria,[33] where they behaved with such brutality that even the Germans, no believers at the time in human rights, were said to be appalled. There could be no more damning commentary than theirs.

After the defeat of Axis came the communists who endured for forty years. They were brutal enough, though perhaps not quite to the extent of their predecessors, but in aggregate they caused suffering almost as great. They had nothing to recommend them and ruined everything they touched. But, by imposing their rule for so long, they enabled the Romanians to think of their nation solely as victimised and to forget their former perpetrations. By the time of Ceausescu's overthrow (by coup d'état, incidentally, rather than by revolution, though the coup unintentionally revolutionised

---

[33] Actually, the occupation of Bessarabia was the recovery of Romanian sovereign territory that had been Romanian since the end of the First World War. This was reasonable enough because the population was Romanian. It was Stalin, after the signing of the Molotov-Ribbentrop pact, who demanded by ultimatum cession of the territory to the Soviet Union, thus ensuring the entry of Romania into the war on the German side.

Romanian society and history), you would have had to have been in your late fifties at the youngest to have any real adult memory of the pre-communist regime; all you would have known was communism. And so, as soon as the subject of the Romanian war record came up, it was open to Romanians to say, 'Yes, but what about communism?' — as if atrocities could be justified by what came after them. Moreover, communism had the merit, from the point of view of self-exculpation, of having been imposed on the country from outside and would never have taken hold were it not for the Soviet Union. Before the imposition of communist rule, the Romanian Communist Party was tiny. Romanian fascism, by contrast, was a home-grown product and accorded much better with the national spirit of the times.

This film — *Who Cares If History Considers Us Barbarians* — is an attempt (I think) to encourage Romanians to face up to their past. There has recently been a tendency in Romania to rehabilitate the memory of the wartime dictator, Marshal Antonescu, so clearly the makers of the film would like to counter this dangerous current of revisionism. It raises many interesting and important questions whose answers, or attempted answers, could fill a book, or a library of books.

In the film, a young theatre director wants to mount a kind of theatrical tableau of Romania's part in the Second World War. To this end, she assembles a large group of people, none of them professional actors. The tableau is to be mounted in the very centre of Bucharest before an audience that includes the mayor of the city who is a woman with a traditionally and uncritically patriotic view of the past. I recognised the location, just in front of the *Athenée Palace* hotel, made famous by Olivia Manning's *Balkan Trilogy* and the subject, or rather the location, of a wonderful book by the Countess Waldeck, describing with brilliant clarity the byzantine intrigues that went on in it in the years up to the beginning of the war. The recognition of a location that most people in the (small) audience probably didn't recognise was, of course, a singular pleasure, that of my own superior knowledge or acquaintance.

The film begins slowly and not very impressively. The character of the director is not sympathetic at first because of her self-righteousness. But she has interesting discussions with a fellow intellectual who argues that her tableau will be inopportune or even counterproductive. Why not, he asks, choose another subject, for example the prison labour camps organised by the communists in which thousands were killed or worked to death? The director agrees that these too are suitable subjects; it is just that they are not hers at the moment. Another interlocutor asks her how she can inculpate or condemn a whole nation, to which she replies that if, as a patriot, she is proud of her nation's achievements, of its great men, is it not also morally necessary or honest that she should acknowledge what is less glorious, indeed is outright criminal, in its past? You can't have Brancusi and Ionesco, say, without Codreanu (founder and leader of the vicious Iron Guard).

This is a problem that affects practically all countries. There must be very few whose history is without blemish or dark episode, and if any such exist it would be rather a manifestation of their weakness rather than of their goodness. With the advance of tertiary education — not an unmixed blessing, I think — patriotic history, in which the country's past is related as a ceaseless upward trajectory or a succession of great figures, with only minor setbacks caused by traitors and foreigners, no longer satisfies anyone. It is a fairy tale and is now seen as such. No longer can the less glorious aspects of a country's history be written off as mere aberration. The danger is that of a gestalt switch, such that now a country's history is seen as a chain of disaster without achievement, a mirror image of the patriotic version. This in turn produces a patriotic reaction, so that there is a constant oscillation between self-abasement and self-glorification, neither of which is healthy. Of all things balance is the most difficult to achieve and seldom lasts long.

By far the most arresting part of the film — and it is very arresting indeed — is the scene of the tableau when, after having overcome various obstacles, the director succeeds in mounting it in central Bucharest. The temporary actors have been divided into four bands, the Nazis, the Romanians, the Soviets and the Jews. The first three are in military uniforms; only the last are civilians. First the Nazis appear, marching to oom-pah-pah music, to which the gathered audience claps happily in time. The Nazis are popular with the crowd. Their uniforms are handsome, and they appear well-disciplined.

The Nazis are followed by the Soviets, also in uniform, but dowdy and ill-fitting. They make much less of a spectacle than the Nazis, and the audience hisses and boos them, as Victorian audiences hissed and booed the villain of a melodrama.

Then come the Romanians in army uniform. They raise the Romanian tricolor — red, yellow and blue — to tremendous cheering from the crowd. The Patriarch of the Romanian Orthodox Church comes to bless them in their holy endeavour to recover Bessarabia from the Russians. In the process of blessing the troops, the Patriarch utters violently antisemitic sentiments with which the crowd obviously sympathise.

A mock battle ensues in which the Romanian army confronts the Soviets and drives them from the field. Marshal Antonescu addresses the troops and gives orders that the Jews of Moldavia, Transnistria and Odessa are to be exterminated, a task that the Romanian troops perform joyfully. (Antonescu, inconsistently enough, ordered that the 350,000 Jews living within the borders of Romania as it existed in 1940 *not* be killed, such that a higher proportion of Jews living in that part of Romania survived the war than in any other country in Nazi-dominated Europe, with the exception of Denmark, while they had the lowest chance of survival in the other parts).

After the initial triumph of the Romanians over the Soviets — destined to be short-lived, of course, once the Germans lose — the tableau shows the Romanians rounding up the Jews and herding them into a wooden shed. One of the Jews tries to escape and runs into the audience that is watching. In perhaps the most dramatic, and certainly the most horrifying, scene in the film, the audience (who have thoroughly suspended their disbelief) spontaneously block the escape of the Jew and violently return him to the Romanian soldiers who are trying to recapture him. The escape, it goes without saying, was part of the tableau's script, a test of the audience, and the reaction of the audience suggests that nothing much has changed in the Romanian mentality since the 1930s. How far this is fair or accurate I cannot say.

Then the wooden shed into which the Jews have been herded is set alight and they are burned to death. The final scene is of a collective scaffold for Jews, represented by mannikins. At last the audience is subdued by the horror of this spectacle, and the film ends with the director saying to her fellow intellectuals that she is now moving on to her next project, a theatrical adaptation of a story by Chekhov.

In his speech to the troops, the Patriarch quotes Nicolae Paulescu, Romania's greatest physiologist, also a virulent anti-Semite who had the good fortune (from the point of view of his posthumous reputation) to die in 1931, well before the worst of what was to happen. The Patriarch quotes:

> Can we exterminate them [the Jews] just as, for instance, bedbugs are killed? This would be the simplest and easiest way of getting rid of them.

What the Patriarch does not quote, however, for very discreditable reasons, is Paulescu's answer to his own question:

> But no! We must never even think of such a thing… we must love the Jews and do them good because we have Christ as our teacher… who in his divine wisdom said, Love your enemies, do good to them that hate you.

Still, all this talk of enmity, bedbugs and extermination suggests that genocide was in the Romanian *air du temps* as a genuine possibility, even in Paulescu's day.

When we left the cinema, my wife and I discussed the question of whether it was best to rake over old history, dwell on it, or let sleeping dogs (in the form of old hatreds) lie. I suppose it depends on the spirit in which it is done:

recrimination, self-flattery, the search for political advantage, or a genuine desire for self-examination and to learn from the past.

32

BAGHDAD STATION, DIR. MOHAMED AL DARADJI, IRAQ

This is a film about Iraq in the aftermath of the Second Gulf War. Sometimes a little mannered, it is nevertheless very powerful. In the week in which I saw it, however, it was shown only once, at eleven thirty on a Saturday morning. Apart from my wife, there were only three other people in the audience. The epidemiology, so to speak, of public taste is interesting.

I should put my cards on the table with regard to the Second Gulf War. In my opinion it was probably a criminal, and certainly a stupid, enterprise.[34] It was fought on a trumped-up pretext in which few of any intelligence seriously believed. There was no evidence whatsoever then that Iraq was responsible for the attack on the World Trade Center, and there never has been any since. That Saddam Hussein was a murderous monster, psychopathic from an early age, was true,

---

[34] *C'est pire qu'un crime, c'est une faute* (It's worse than a crime, it's a mistake): this is usually attributed to Talleyrand, but it was really Antoine Claude Joseph Boulay de la Meurthe who said it, on learning of the summary execution of the Duc d'Enghien in 1804.

but the war was fought with very little thought of what might or ought to come afterwards. Ridding the world of monsters is not enough to make it safe. Did anyone truly believe that after the 'liberation,' Iraq would settle down to Scandinavian-style democracy and become the Denmark of the Middle East? Did anyone believe that the Sunni and Shia Arabs were thirsting to share power equitably between them, let alone with the Kurds, to become a showcase of multiculturalism? Did anyone not spot that, in a war supposedly directed at Islamist terrorism and violence, an enemy was selected who was one of the few secularist leaders in the region, as the result of whose downfall the two-millennial history of Christianity in the country would come almost to an end? Did anyone really not notice that the nidus of Islamic extremism lay elsewhere, precisely in those countries in which the West in general and the United States in particular had their most powerful economic interests? President Chirac of France, who warned against the war and was a man as morally flexible as Talleyrand, was derided at the time by many Americans as being the leader of a nation of *cheese-eating surrender monkeys*, though few would now deny that he was right and few would advocate the war again if they had the chance to start afresh.

Well! In the film we see a young woman who has decided to become a suicide-bomber. Her target is the Baghdad Central Station on the day of its re-opening after the end of the conventional war. We see nothing of the process by which she has been indoctrinated into sacrificing herself in this way; we see only that she has a face of stone, a complete lack of flexibility and the tone, when she speaks, of a robot or automaton. I have witnessed this transformation of men into machines, or at least the appearance of machines, elsewhere, in North Korea for example. Only certain kinds of ideas have the capacity to do this (usually backed by threat), and severe forms of Islam clearly are among them. In this case, Islam is linked to outraged national feeling against the American occupation: national Islamism, so to speak, rather than national socialism.

We know nothing of her background, but she is clearly intelligent and probably educated. Sometimes you have to be educated to believe in idiocies such as suicide bombing followed by an ascent to paradise, though what, as a female, the protagonist's reward would be in place of seventy-two virgins (perhaps she would become one of them?) was unclear.

She is ready to explode herself when she hesitates and in that moment is approached by a young man, handsome but frivolous, a seducer and petty swindler, who is waiting in the station for a consignment of used limb prostheses which he will try to sell as new. It is not easy to believe that he would be successful in this dubious endeavour, but the film reminds us repeatedly that these are not normal times.

Among other things, whether intentionally or not, the film demonstrates that the Iraq of Saddam Hussein had been in some respects — of what importance is a matter of debate — a functioning country. Some of the action takes place in the shunting yards just beyond the station, where many ruined or decaying locomotives and railway carriages stand rotting further. Until the war, they actually worked and on quite a large scale.

The film is certainly not an apology for the Saddam regime, however. A tiny vignette lets us know just how horrible it was.

A group of musicians, buskers, plays in the station. (Incidentally, how much more civilised and refined is Arab popular music than its Western rock equivalent!) One of the musicians both sings and plays the clarinet, both rather beautifully and with a decidedly melancholy timbre. We learn from a short scene that the woman who has waited for him while he spent twenty-two years in prison wants to marry him, but he says that he cannot afford to, being only an itinerant musician. We know that his imprisonment could not have been morally justified by anything he had done and that he must have suffered horrible abuse during it. You don't have to know much about Iraq to know that. Such was the Saddam regime.

The would-be suicide bomber takes her attempted seducer hostage, threatening to blow him up if he does not do exactly what she tells him. (She has shown him the explosives strapped to her body.) We see the desperation of life in Iraq after the war through scenes in the station. Itinerant children, orphans, try to make a living by shining shoes or selling flowers. There is no honour among orphans, and as soon as any of them has a little money, a band of them relieves him of it by force. One is reminded of *Lord of the Flies*. Nor do any of the adults take pity on the orphans: they swat them away as though they were noisome insects. One is quick to be appalled and then to condemn, but given how quickly we lose our temper over minor inconvenience, we soon realise that, horrible as is the behaviour towards these children by adults, we might not react so very differently in similar circumstances.

There are a few scenes in which American soldiers appear. They are portrayed in an unflattering, but I am afraid quite plausible, way. They are, of course, chronically frightened. They are patrolling in a city whose language they do not speak and whose people for the most part hate them. They could at any moment be the object of an attack and have no idea who is who. Any woman in a black robe could be a suicide bomber: not to be paranoid here would be foolhardy. Yet even allowing for this they are unattractive, their main idea of human interaction with the locals being to *kick ass*, to use an expression that somehow lacks charm. Their manner is coarse and crude, and one suspects that it is not only because they are lowly members of the army doing work that would be terribly boring if it were not terrifying and that, moreover, is without obvious connection to the vital interests of their country, being more a political vanity project. If their manner is coarse and crude, it reflects that of their own culture.

They are not the only ones who are paranoid, however: relations between Iraqis are hardly any better. The Saddam experience and then the war has turned everyone fearful of everyone else.[35] But one Iraqi Christian doctor whom I met, a refugee in England, told me that life under Saddam had been tolerable on two conditions: that you did not concern yourself with politics and, if you were in business, that you did not try to muscle in on any areas of business in which Saddam or his proteges and clientele were interested. Christians were not particularly persecuted by Saddam as they soon were under

---

[35] A well-known book about Saddam's Iraq was titled *The Republic of Fear*.

the new, supposedly more democratic dispensation[36], and while the two rules just cited were not fully compliant with the Universal Declaration of Human Rights, at least you knew where you were under them. Subsequently, there were no rules whatsoever (said my informant), and an arbitrary death lurked anywhere and everywhere. Anarchy was worse than tyranny, though Iraqi Kurds might demur.

A woman in the station suddenly hands a bag to the suicide bomber and her hostage. (The suicide bomber is now a hostage of her hostage, since she cannot let him go for fear he will inform on her before she has managed to kill as large a number of people — unbelievers — as possible.) Shortly afterwards, they hear a baby's cry emerge from the bag. It is the beginning of the re-humanisation of the suicide bomber. At first the man has a more protective attitude towards the baby: her first reaction is to abandon it. But gradually she has, or allows, a more human response to invade her and the brittle carapace of her ideology begins to crack. Finally, she realises, thanks to the baby, that she is on the side of life rather than of death.

Now, however, she has another problem: she does not know how to disencumber herself of the suicide belt she is wearing without setting it off. Her former hostage, with whom she is probably half-falling in love, says he knows someone, an electronics expert, who could disconnect the explosives. They are now nearly a couple, and they manage to return the baby

---

[36] Freedom and democracy are not the same and can even be opposed.

to its mother, who has thought better of abandoning it, having done so only because it was born illegitimate. They experience a few adventures such as taking a train to Mosul (which was not, in the near future, a safe destination), but the train is the object of a suicide bomb attack that derails it and leaves many dead and injured. They have to flee the organization that has trained her to blow herself up — if training is quite the word for it — and at the end of the film they take refuge overnight in an empty, ruined mosque. When she wakes in the morning, the man has deserted her: she is now back on her own, as she was at the beginning of the film, the difference being that she no longer wants to blow herself up. How, or even whether, she rids herself of her explosive belt remains unknown at the end of the film.

What she says, however, when she wakes in the old mosque and her former hostage, now companion, has crept away, is both ambivalent and significant. 'You have deceived me,' she says. But who is it that has deceived her? Is it the young man, is it the people who persuaded her to become a suicide bomber, or is it God Himself? Or perhaps all three? Is it Islam rather than God? This is a possible interpretation, though no doubt the director would disavow it because of the consequences of not doing so. It is unlikely that an anti-Islamic message was included in the proposal to make it. But at the same time, no possible pro-Islamic message could be derived from it. When, early in the film, the suicide bomber says that she is acting to save religion, no argument is offered that what she proposes to do is actually *against* religion.

The portrayal of life in Baghdad after the foreign invasion is very strong and very depressing. It certainly does not have the air of propaganda about it, but of reality. No one comes out of it well, except possibly the clarinet player. Those who seek to purify the world, either by ridding it of dictators or of the impiety of the great mass of humanity, only make it more unbearable than it was before. Schemes of perfection are stupid, because life is not perfectible.

33

COMPAÑEROS, DIR. ÁLVARO BRECHNER, URUGUAY

Western European and North American intellectuals long admired, supported and perhaps even envied Latin American guerrillas who seemed to have the courage, and often the brutality, of their convictions. They projected on to the Latin American poor all the virtues of the noble savage and on to the guerrilla leaders all those of the authentic, selfless, revolutionary intellectual. This produced a state of mind that might be characterised as guerrillophilia, the belief that anyone who takes up arms against an incumbent government must be morally superior to that government, and that such moral superiority, by itself, justifies their actions. And it is true, of course, that most Latin American governments in history have not themselves been a spectacle of moral grandeur, not from the very advent of independence from Spain.

In the 1970s, the countries of the Southern Cone fell under the rule of military dictatorship — Argentina, Chile and Uruguay. Of the three, that of Chile is hated the most by Western European and North American intellectuals, though it is not clear that it was the worst in the scale of its brutality. The reason for the hatred, perhaps, is that, alone of the three, it actually achieved something besides the killing of a lot of people. It left the country in a state of economic prosperity by pursuing policies directly opposite to those advocated by those intellectuals who took an interest in Latin American affairs, and therefore committed the unforgivable sin of proving them wrong. The economic success of Chile humiliated the intellectuals, whereas the military dictatorships of Argentina and Uruguay left nothing behind but economic chaos and therefore posed no threat to the intellectuals' worldview. Hence the differential in hatred.

This film is a graphic reconstruction of the treatment by the Uruguayan dictatorship of three prominent Tupamaros after their capture. The Tupamaros were a Uruguayan urban guerrilla movement that sought to overthrow the government and then pursue socialist policies. It was less bloodthirsty than some — most — Latin American guerrilla movements, but it nevertheless did not hesitate to employ violence — kidnap and assassination — even if its violence was more carefully targeted than was customary among such guerrilla movements. It took its name from Tupac Amaru, the Amerindian leader in Peru of a revolt against the Spanish colonisers: somewhat ironically, since the leaders of the movement could not have been more European in descent, as indeed were the vast majority of Uruguayans.

The three Tupamaros of the film were Elanterio Fernández Huidobro, José Mújica, and Mauricio Rosencof, who later became, respectively: Senator; Minister of Defence and President of the Republic; and theatre director, playwright and Montevideo's adviser on cultural matters. They were held together in various military prisons in Uruguay, though each in solitary confinement that lasted twelve years. The treatment meted out to them was abominable beyond description.

The film starts *in medias res*, with the three headed off to prison and then to dungeon. We do not see what they had done to merit their incarceration, nor are we told that Mújica had already escaped more than once, which might explain (in small part) the exceptional measures to detain him and his associates in so strict a way. A film or play has to start somewhere, and if we demand a context, someone else might demand a context of a context, and so on until the Garden of Eden. Nevertheless, the lack of context in this case was bound to increase, and was almost certainly intended to increase, the sympathy for the three men, because all we learn of them is their suffering at the hands of brutes.

The scenes of maltreatment that lasted for years are hard to watch, because they are intensely realistic and (one assumes) very close to what actually happened or rather was done by their captors. The three were not only kept in the most frightful conditions but subjected to many kinds of torture, from being made to stand for hours to near suffocation by wet cloths, from electric shocks to (perhaps the worst and most cruel of all) bombardment by noise, including recordings of voices to drive them mad — which, in one case, it did, if only temporarily. This was done from sheer sadistic malice: neither increased security for the country nor the obtaining of more information about the Tupamaros could have been its purpose. Here was what Coleridge mistakenly attributed to Iago, motiveless malignity, that is to say malignity for its own sake, as an end in itself. I do not think that most people will have to look far into their hearts to know that the infliction of suffering on others can be a pleasure all of itself, and is the more dangerous when there is supposedly some kind of justification for it, such as the defence of the father- or motherland.

The first part of the film is so unremittingly horrible that my wife who was with me wanted to leave. There is, of course, a fine line to be drawn between the educative display of the gruesome and the voyeuristic wallowing in it. Should one avoid representations of the most appalling inhumanity? Is such avoidance the evasion of one's duty to know, or a proper and decent tact and reliance on the implicit?

For myself, I do not see how anyone could derive any pleasure, no matter how illicit, from the portrayal of the treatment to which these three men were subjected, and from the point of view of artistic effect such portrayal had to be prolonged (albeit on the cinematographic timescale) in order to convey the sheer unrelenting duration of the maltreatment: a brief episode would not have been enough. The depiction was very far from the stylised variety seen in commercial Hollywood films: this was more the kind of violence whose results one sees in the emergency department of an inner-city hospital, which have nothing stylish or glamorous about them but is merely repellent and sordid.

The film, I presume, was made with a predominantly Uruguayan audience in mind, perhaps Argentinian also, to be taken as a salutary reminder of the ease with which civilized behaviour can be replaced by savagery, even in a generally peaceful country once known as the Switzerland of South America.

Humankind cannot bear very much reality, not even in the

cinema. If we cannot bear an hour's depiction on the screen, how should we survive it for real? Perhaps, in some cases, the ability increases with necessity to do so.

Gradually, very slowly, the conditions under which the prisoners are kept are alleviated. One of them, Rosencof, even forges some kind of relationship with a sergeant who, having heard that he was a writer, asks him to write love letters on his behalf since he is himself only semi-literate. When Rosencof complies, they say thank you to one another, a great advance over the early years of the imprisonment, when the gaolers were not allowed to address even a single word to the prisoners.

While the three are moved from one prison to another, blindfolded, one of them, having seen nothing but the inside of cells for several years, is now even allowed to remove his blindfold and catch a glimpse of the countryside. The ecstasy with which, after so long a captivity, he looks on the world is well, plausibly and movingly portrayed: we almost feel the ecstasy with him. How little we appreciate what we have until we have lost it! I was reminded of W. E. Henley's poem, *Discharged*, one of his twenty hospital poems that he wrote in response to his eighteen-month bedbound stay in the Edinburgh Royal Infirmary, where Joseph Lister treated his ankle for tuberculosis, until then untreatable, and saved his leg from amputation, his other leg having been already amputated. His ecstasy on leaving the hospital is of the same order as that of the Tupamaro catching a glimpse of the countryside:

Carry me out
Into the wind and the sunshine,
Into the beautiful world.

O, the wonder, the spell of the streets!

Whether artfully or not, a couple of the most important lines in the film are uttered so fleetingly, so much *en passant*, that the inattentive viewer or listener might miss them. Confronted by one of his tormentors, the army officer who had captured him years earlier, one of the guerrillas says that he acknowledges his mistakes and is prepared to take his punishment for them. Of course, by his mistakes he means his crimes, for one is not punished for mere mistakes, though reality might make one pay for them. But this acknowledgement that he is not wholly innocent is both important and impressive, for it is also an acknowledgement that, if he had not been captured and detained, he almost certainly would have continued to make his 'mistakes', to the great detriment not only of himself and his victims but of the country as a whole. The Tupamaros' cause was good neither as to ends nor means.

But nothing could justify the way in which they were treated. Nevertheless, it is well that they were detained for a long time, because their repentance was a slow process rather than a sudden conversion. They should have been treated humanely, as everyone should be treated humanely, and if they had been so treated, perhaps their repentance would have come the quicker.

We see them leaving prison after twelve years and are glad

for them. Their survival, psychological as much as physical, is remarkable, a triumph of the human spirit. Later (though the film ends well before this), they re-join political life by strictly legal means and are very successful. It is beside the point whether or not they pursue wise policies: they have learnt that kidnapping and assassination are not a justified means to anything and were not justified when they employed them.

I have long been no admirer of Latin American guerrilla movements. They are the expression of the discontent of the university-educated rather than that of the peasantry or proletariat. They are a consequence of social mobility rather than of its absence. But this film was a lesson not so much in how to forgive — one can forgive only those who have harmed one — as in how not to let one's prior hostility entirely guide one's response to changed situations by refusal to recognise change. By all accounts, President Mújica is now an avuncular figure, free of corruption, modest in his manner, and much loved. It would have been very different if he had become president nearly fifty years earlier: then he would have been reviled long ago. Thus, there is a message of hope in this film.

Made in the USA
Columbia, SC
26 March 2021

35122322R00159